London's Ley Lines

Pathways of Enlightenment

By

Chris Street

Earthstars Publishing
London N14 6LP

By the same Author:

Earthstars (1990) Hermitage Publishing

Earthstars The Visionary Landscape (2000) Hermitage Publishing

The Beer Guru's Guide (2006) Souvenir press

London's Camelot and The Secrets of The Grail (2009)
Earthstars Publishing

London's Camelot is available from www.lulu.com, as a paperback or downloadable e-book. See www.earthstars.co.uk for availability of the other titles.

© 2010 Earthstars Publishing (formerly Hermitage Publishing) and C. Street.

Christopher Street has asserted his right to be identified as the author of this work in accordance with the Copyright, Designs and Patents Act 1988.

A CIP catalogue record for this book is available from The British Library.

ISBN: 978-0-9515967-4-6

First published, March 21st 2010.

"The instrument of all human enlightenment
is an educated mind, illuminated by revelation."

John Michell

Contents

"Human life is enriched by means of a force activated through the correct geographical relationship of sacred centres."

John Michell

Illustrations

Illustrations continued

Part One

Leys - a Personal Perspective

Introduction

Hidden Knowledge

Leys are as elusive as beams of starlight. They are everywhere. You just can't see them.

On the other hand, evidence for their existence as linear alignments of old churches and other ancient sites, is freely available to anyone with a ruler and Ordnance Survey map, or the inclination to climb to the viewing platform atop St. Paul's dome (or some other vantage point) and see for themselves how well some of the capital's church spires and towers line up.

Like many of the mysteries of nature, they are an open secret, on public display, for anyone willing to investigate and decipher their enigmas. Trouble is, if you don't know what to look for, you would never suspect they exist at all.

Thus, Leys maybe compared to the hidden knowledge of a secret tradition. Freely available to those in the know. Totally invisible to those who aren't.

Indeed, there is much in the nature of leys and their associations to suggest that, at various times in the past, this was literally the case.

The basis of this knowledge is of immense antiquity. That is certain.

Where remnants of our most ancient sacred sites and monuments still remain, as standing stones, stone circles, earthwork henges, sacred wells, old churches, abbeys or cathedrals, there is always ample evidence that they form key mark points in linear alignments.

In fact, in his ground-breaking work, **The View Over Atlantis**, the world's leading visionary scholar on this subject, the late John Michell, demonstrates beyond a shadow of a doubt that:

" We all live within the ruins of an ancient structure, whose vast size has hitherto rendered it invisible. The entire surface of the Earth is marked with the traces of a gigantic work of prehistoric engineering, the remains of a once universal system of natural magic involving the use of polar magnetism together with another positive force related to solar energy."

" Modern research has revealed that the stone monuments of prehistoric antiquity are not the work of primitive barbarians, but are instead the scientific instruments of an advanced universal civilization."

In England, the well-documented tendency of successive cultures to build their temples and churches on existing sacred sites, means that even relatively modern Victorian parish churches built upon Norman or Saxon origins, may mark a site far, far, older, usually connected by one or more alignments to this vast and ancient network.

Leys, therefore, lie at the foundation of our spiritual centres and are connected to the mysteries of what made these spots sacred in the first place.

At certain times in the past, this would not simply have been ancient knowledge or hidden knowledge. It would have been dangerous knowledge.

Leys involve the unknown, the intangible, the invisible, the unprovable and, for some, the unthinkable.

They are a phenomenon defined principally by sacred sites, places which traditionally connect us to our spiritual dimensions, regardless of whatever belief system we embrace.

In the past this would have been understood in a far more literal way than many today would imagine.

To our ancestors, these sites were places of power, places of the gods, places of healing, places of vision, places of mystical experience, initiation, inspiration and revelation. To some, they still are.

For these reasons, any strictly academic or scientific approach to the subject is likely to prove inconclusive or woefully inadequate.

As with all initiatory processes, your own personal intuitive experiences are the key to sensing their reality, relevance and meaning.

Hence this book is designed as a guide to inform, enlighten and inspire you to discover the wonders of leys and their defining sites for yourself.

Even today, the special, numinous nature of these locations can best be sensed in the peace and tranquility of the atmosphere that surrounds them, simply by sitting still and quietly letting the energy and power of the place slowly seep into you.

Unfortunately, the elusive and intangible nature of leys means that the evidence of their existence, disregarded or unnoticed by many, has continually been buried, by JCB, plough or bulldozer, and replaced by acres of rapeseed, miles of paving slabs, tarmac and roads, tower blocks, homes, offices and all the needs of an overpopulated, modern, materialistic society.

That makes tracking them down all the more difficult, particularly in a place like London. Yet even here, enough evidence remains. It is sometimes a little harder to find perhaps, but it still exists.

Rare thought they are, London still has ancient stones and tracks, burial mounds, sacred hills, henges, holy wells and secret shrines, all the usual features, in fact, that mark those elusive leys.

The trick is, not to fall into the trap of seeing leys and their defining sites as something from the distant past, outdated, long dead and part of a system in terminal decay.

If the energy of leys is an expression of the planetary and universal life force, as I believe, you are likely to find that they are very much alive, that the forces of creation flow freely through them and can still be sensed or experienced in a number of ways.

In a Christian sense, they are pathways of the Holy Spirit, a web of divine power between places of worship or sacred celebration. Their origins and essence, of course, are pre-Christian, but many of their current mark points are fully functional as today's local parish churches and their services, prayers, sacred music and bell-ringing all seem to play a role in boosting the energy of the ley system and keep it flowing, just as the rituals and activities of the pre-Christian temples before them did.

As with everything on this small planet, there is evolution.

The ancient wisdom at the basis of leys is still encoded within the land for future generations to discover anew, whatever your religious inclinations or convictions.

London's leys can lead you to magical places, to the soul of the city and to an understanding of the hidden unity which connects our ancient sacred sites to each other and also links our spiritual dimensions to theirs.

These are still places of power, places of the gods, places of healing, vision, mystical experience, initiation, inspiration and revelation.

More important, they are places you can visit and experience for yourself.

Anytime you like.

Chapter One

The Beginning of Leys

The first book about ley alignments appeared in 1925, **The Old Straight Track**, researched and written by Alfred Watkins, a Herefordshire businessman.

I first read it when I was about sixteen, having borrowed it from the local library at Hall Green in Birmingham, an establishment which seemed to have had an extraordinary collection of mystical tomes, some of them now very rare.

The Old Straight Track, by contrast, is no rarity. Back then, it had already been around for over forty years and now, another forty years later, it is still in print, still a mine of useful information on the subject and still something of a heretical tome to the academic and archaeological communities.

What it demonstrates, beyond a shadow of a doubt, in meticulous detail and with numerous examples, is that certain types of ancient sites: churches, standing stones, earthworks, stone circles, mounds, moats, paths, tracks, hilltops and other landscape features, form perfectly straight alignments across the land, sometimes stretching for many miles.

Watkins initially considered these lines to be the visible remnants of a system of ancient trackways and sighting lines which could only have been surveyed and laid out at some point in extreme antiquity by our distant ancestors.

Unfortunately, the historians and archaeologists of his time did not agree. According to them, Watkins' work was flawed for a variety of reasons:

1; Some of the alignments covered impassable terrain, improbable for a realistic track of any sort.

2; The leys' various mark points were often dated to different periods and so, they assumed, could not be connected, by alignments or anything else.

3; They regarded our ancestors as a bunch of uneducated, woad-splattered, bog-hopping troglodytes, bereft of any surveying skills and incapable of such an achievement.

Thus, very early on, the evidence for any kind of leys was dismissed and the subject deemed unworthy of any scholarly attention span, however short.

Baby and bathwater went down the plughole of academia and it was left to members of Watkins' Old Straight Track Club and other Ley Hunters, to carry on their research, which they did with great enthusiasm.

In those early years, a huge amount of evidence was gathered for the existence of these alignments and even more has been amassed since.

As John Michell stated in **The View over Atlantis** in 1973:

"His claim that he had seen the whole country covered by a network of straight lines linking the centres and sites of antiquity, seemed incredible, but such was the quality of the evidence produced that it was impossible to dismiss without further inquiry."

Watkins' extensive research into the phenomenon laid a very firm foundation for the future investigation of leys and gave those who followed him a wealth of information to work with.

It amounts to enough material to convince anyone, except those with the most firmly closed minds, that there is definitely something here worth investigating.

However, whether leys exist is only half the problem.

As Danny Sullivan writes in his study of the phenomenon, a comprehensive book modestly titled **Ley Lines**: *" Watkins would not have been satisfied with proof that they simply existed; he wanted to know why they existed."*

Unfortunately, a scientifically proven, full and definitive understanding of what they actually represent, was never accepted in Watkin's lifetime.

Any personal understanding of leys that he or other members of the Old Straight Track Club developed, could only be regarded as an informed subjective opinion or personal theory.

That generally remains the case to the present day. The subject is still a source of enormous controversy.

Ask a dozen people what leys are and you will probably be treated to a dozen different answers; some of them reasonable and fairly credible; some, seemingly bonkers.

Here are a few of the ideas that have been thrown into the fray for consideration, over the years.

Fairy paths, death roads, sacred roads or holy ways, merchants' trackways, shamanic flight paths, acupuncture meridians of the Earth, Feng Shui dragon paths, song lines, salt roads, electromagnetic force lines, planetary soul lines, pathways of collective consciousness, currents of the universal and planetary life force, spirit paths.

If nothing else, they serve to illustrate why the subject of leys is so difficult for orthodox, rational thinkers to accept and why it is such an easy target for the kind of sarcasm and shallow wit normally reserved for trainspotters and Guardian readers.

Seemingly, leys can be many things to many people.

That's the beauty of the ill-defined. If you don't know for certain what it is, it can be whatever you think it is.

Whether it is correct or not, the popular concept of a "ley line" prevalent since the sixties, seems to incorporate and embrace several of the more imaginative concepts.

It is usually conceived as a line of mysterious "Earth energy," possibly electromagnetic in nature, but also somehow a psychic and spiritual force, related to the fundamental life-force of the planet and universe.

The places that mark an alignment are conceived as node points in this energy matrix and therefore, must be places of numinous power, which is why they are so often sacred sites.

Leys, whatever they are in physical terms, have an undeniable, mystical and spiritual element which adds to the confusion.

For those ley-hunters who longed for their research and work to gain academic acceptance and recognition, it has been a curse that prevented the subject from ever being taken seriously, except as something to de-bunk.

For the mystics, psychics, dowsers, druids, wiccans, spiritual seekers, neo-pagans, new-age light workers, spliff-heads, travellers and hippies of all eras, the mystical element of leys was a godsend, or in some cases, a goddess-send, adding some interesting, new, personal experiences to their already unorthodox lives.

However, the subject of leys did not suddenly go hippy-dippy in the flower-power sixties. It just looked that way. This mystic element had been there from the very beginning.

Even before Watkins published his findings, German researchers were investigating similar alignments and calling them "Holy Lines" because they linked sacred sites and were predominantly defined by them.

The way in which Alfred Watkins' discovery of leys came about is singularly relevant to their mystical nature and indicative of their possible effects on the human psyche. It was not something he deliberately set out to discover. It came to him in a sudden flash of inspiration.

According to the foreword by John Michell in the Abacus edition of **The Old Straight Track**, reprinted for the umpteenth time in 1976:

" the revelation took place when Watkins was sixty five years old. Riding across the hills near Bredwardine in his native county, he pulled up his horse to look out over the landscape below. At that moment he became aware of a network of lines, standing out like glowing wires all over the surface of the country, intersecting at the sites of churches, old stones and other spots of traditional sanctity. The vision is not recorded in The Old Straight Track, but throughout his life, Watkins privately maintained that he had perceived the existence of the Ley system in a single flash and, for all his subsequent study, he added nothing to his conviction, save only the realization of the particular significance of beacon hills as terminal points in the alignments."

Mr Michell expands on the experience on page 21 of **The View over Atlantis**:

"Watkins saw straight through the surface of the landscape to a layer deposited in some remote prehistoric age. The barrier of time

melted away and, spread across the country, he saw a web of lines linking holy places and sites of antiquity. Mounds, old stones, crosses and old crossroads, churches placed on pre-Christian sites, legendary trees, moats and holy wells stood in exact alignments that ran over beacon hills to cairns and mountain peaks. In one moment of transcendant perception, Watkins entered the magic world of prehistoric Britain, a world whose very existence had been forgotten."

Some researchers, possibly alarmed that this disclosure could invoke the mystic ley curse to the detriment of their reputations, have gone to great pains to explain what a practical and down-to-earth man Alfred Watkins was. Beyond a shadow of a doubt, they were correct.

He was definitely not a head-in-the-clouds fantasist, prone to frequent visions or flights of fancy.

Yet the fact remains, that what he experienced was a vision of sorts. My theory is that it has as much to do with the place as the man.

Ancient sacred sites are notorious for these things.

Dr. James Swan, in his book, **Sacred Places**, recounts how an unexpected visionary experience in Dakota's Black Hills prompted a personal path of discovery that has made him something of an authority in this unusual field.

Dr. Swan has collected hundreds of case histories of people who have had extraordinary experiences at sacred sites.

The most common occurrences have included feelings of ecstasy, joy or unification with nature, profound dreams, feeling unusual energies, and hearing either words, voices, music or song.

My own personal experiences over the last twenty years, working with the notion of "spirit of place" and the Earthstars discovery (which came as much as a revelation to me, as anyone else), prompts

10

me to add an idea of my own to the lengthy list of suggestions concerning what leys might be.

I am beginning to think of them as paths of enlightenment.

Paths that can lead you, through personal experience and intiatory processes, to a form of gnosis, an understanding of the knowledge and wisdom encoded in the Earth and its sacred sites.

**"Anyone who has followed their paths across country
will find that his life has been enriched,
perhaps deepened,
by the experience."**

John Michell

Chapter Two

Paths of Enlightenment

A study of leys leads you to many other areas of knowledge connected to these alignments and their mark sites. It brings you into contact with subjects, variously esoteric or anomalous.

If you are blessed, it treats you to unusual experiences, so your understanding of things weird and wonderful grows daily, through the osmosis of inspiration, revelation or intuition.

Hardly surprising then that these things can evolve into a personal path of enlightenment, or gnosis.

You learn to delve into the dust of ancient history and archaeology. You uncover local folklore, myth and legend.

You learn to read maps. Then pore over them prior to yomping off to whichever destination has exerted its magical attraction over you.

Out in the landscape, you'll find evidence that is marked on no map, like churchyard paths and gates which align perfectly to the route of a ley, allowing you, the otherwise intangible line and its invisible travellers to pass through.

Invariably, you will find ancient trees, churchyard oaks and yews, with such presence you can easily understand why our ancestors venerated them.

You begin to understand the sacred geometry of creation concealed within religious architecture, prehistoric monuments and everywhere in the entire natural world, from the smallest atom to the perfect form of a galactic spiral.

You start to recognize the hidden symbolism in religious architecture, art and artifacts. You find the pagan hidden within the Christian; "Green Men" and "Sheila-Na-Gigs" carved in pews and stone, peering at you from their hiding places in our oldest churches. You discover Templar and Masonic connections.

You may be beset by synchronicities (meaningful coincidences) so that you suspect a hidden helping hand in your explorations. At times, you'll suspect there's a guiding spirit of the leys.

There is. In fact there are two.

Mercurius or Hermes, the Quicksilver Messenger is one. There's also a goddess of the paths, known in Wales as Sarn Elen or Helen of the Ways, an aspect of the Earth Spirit and a wandering goddess of dawn and dusk. (Elen's legend is contained in the **Mabinogion** as **The Dream of Maxen Wledig**).

You may experience sensations of hidden energy and dabble with the art of dowsing, either with angle rods or a pendulum.

You can't fail to notice the atmosphere in certain places. Some, so serene, uplifting and healing. Others, a bit buzzy and over-active.

While you're soaking up the atmosphere (and I recommend that you spend a good few minutes doing this wherever you go), you may experience any of the anomalous phemonena documented by Dr. James Swan.

In London churches, I have personally heard singing when there was no-one else in the building, seen spectral figures, felt energies and angelic presences, heard high-pitched buzzing, seen doors open and shut with no one passing through and had odd balls of light and other strange effects appear on my photographs.

Eventually, the realization may dawn on you that leys are not part of this world. They belong to another dimension of our existence:

13

a visionary landscape that exists alongside our material world, perceived only by those with a certain amount of psychic sensitivity, yet undetectable by any scientific apparatus.

In a flash of gnosis, you may realize it is a landscape where the Earth is animated by a numinous force reminiscent of Alfred Watkins' initial vision: a vast web of life that breathes vitality into all things.

Where trees can talk.

Where birds and other animals are messengers of the gods.

Where the goddess of the ways floats wispily along her paths as a spectral white lady to guide you forward on your journey.

Within this visionary landscape, leys are lines of spirit through which maybe accessed many impulses:

The Forces of Creation.

The Universal Life fFrce.

The Planetary Collective Unconscious.

The Earth Spirit.

The Human Collective Unconscious.

The Community Spirit.

The Soul of a City.

A layer of human emotions.

Spirits or souls, disincarnate and unborn, some arriving to incarnate here, some ascending back to the stars.

It is a universal matrixand it is not a new development.

It is how people saw the world hundreds of years ago, before motorways, Brent Cross, the Canary Wharf tower, high-density housing and Arndale Shopping Centres.

In his book, **The Earth Spirit, its Ways, its Shrines, its Mysteries**, John Michell explains this mystical dimension in terms of an ancient paradigm which suggested that the alignments were *"Pathways of The Earth Spirit"* the animating force of nature which had been perceived by our ancestors as a female deity, The Earth Goddess or Mother Earth, also known to the Alchemists as the Anima Mundi or World Soul, of which we, of course, are all a part.

" From the earliest times and for the greater part of history, men have believed that the Earth is a living being, animated by a spirit that corresponds to the spirit in men."

"The oldest and deepest element in any religion is the cult of the Earth Spirit in her many aspects."

Moreover, he suggested that leys, megalithic monuments and their associated enigmas were evidence of an ancient geomantic science or art, similar to Feng Shui, that utilised the inherent spiritual energies or life force of the Earth for the mutual benefit of nature and humanity.

According to Feng Shui, the natural energy currents within the Earth are called Lung Mei, or dragon paths.

Unlike leys, they are far from straight. They weave through the landscape like serpents.

Where there are straight alignments in Feng Shui, they are always associated with the power of the Emperor, his palace and his rule over the land. The understanding that emerges from these two concepts is of an underground, serpentine force which can be tapped into at certain power points and controlled or directed through over-ground, linear alignments.

This concurs precisely with the two types of energy leys modern doswers find: meandering underground currents and linear overground flows, many verifiable by obvious alignments of sites.

Since this energy is the universal life force, which the Chinese call Chi, it is a power which can have a beneficial, vitalising effect on the health, happiness and fertility of the landscape as well as its inhabitants.

John Michell refers to the art of manipulating this energy as the oldest form of Alchemy, the joining of Heaven and Earth.

In many ancient cultures, the life-force is represented by a deity, most often a goddess. The shaktis of Hinduism, for example.

The visionaries of the time may not therefore have seen or sensed a manifestation of energy. They may have seen a vision of their deity or some other anthropomorphic being.

When you explore these phenomena, there is always an element of exploring your own spiritual dimensions, as well as those of the visionary landscape around you.

You embark on a journey into the collective psyche which is not just deep within the recesses of your subconscious, but also all around us in the world outside, constituting a mythic landscape populated by the archetypes of our mythology and legends into which we project our own psyche.

Who knows what you will experience and discover, about yourself or the world around you.

The knowledge of the ancients is a living and evolving tradition, buried and encoded within the landscape, to be accessed by future generations who understand the nature of the mysteries.

There are many patterns and plans overlaid one upon the other within the layout of London's sacred sites and leys.

Some are natural, some laid down in Wren's re-building of the city, some dating back to Roman, Saxon or Norman eras, some to the time of the Druids, some a natural matrix inherent to the Earth's quintessential structure.

In some instances, the creation of these alignments and geomantic plans were clearly part of the process of taking over the control and rule of the country through its ancient power centres, by invading cultures like the Romans and Normans.

For others, it was sacred work in which the alignments and the patterns they form, were acknowledged as a circuit diagram which carries an inherent spiritual power and beneficial influence to the landscape and its populace.

It's clear though that an understanding of these matters has passed down the centuries as hidden knowledge.

When you look at the geometric gardens, grand avenues and alignments created by people like Inigo Jones (a prominent Mason) around the stately homes and palaces of the ruling elite, as recently as the 18th century, it is obvious that something akin to western Feng Shui was being employed.

In that era, it was probably inspired by the Renaissance and the Vitruvian re-establishment of the principles of sacred geometry. Other examples are clearly of greater antiquity.

My previous books, **Earthstars** (1990) and **Earthstars The Visionary Landscape** (2000) demonstrate that some of London's most ancient sacred sites were laid out to a precise geometric plan, corresponding directly to the design upon which the megaliths of Stonehenge were built more than three thousand years ago.

Clearly, the priesthood of the megalithic era understood the principles of sacred geometry and its connections to the planetary/universal life force better than we do today.

This knowledge has always been part of the perennial wisdom upon which many civilizations, cities and cultures have been built throughout the ages.

Beneath our city streets, the grand plan of a past Golden Age is still discernible in parts, through the many ley alignments and their mark points which can still be traced within the modern landscape and its monstrous carbuncles of architectural ignorance.

But don't take my word for it. See for yourself.

Walk the leys recommended in the next chapters.

Visit the sites.

Step back in time.

Or even step through the veil.

Experience these things for yourself.

The only proof that can be ultimately convincing to most people is the proof of personal experience.

As they used to say in the X files:

The truth is out there.

Part Two

Alfred Watkins' London Leys

Chapter Three

Alfred Watkins' London Leys

Alfred Watkins only mentioned four London leys in **The Old Straight Track**. Three are listed in his chapter on church leys. The fourth is discussed in his chapter on orientation.

They are well-known to experienced ley-hunters and are good leys to walk (apart from one that crosses the Thames - not even good wellies will get you across that).

You could spend anywhere from a couple of hours to an entire day getting from one end to the other, depending on how long you take to look around each of the mark points en route.

Bear in mind that some of the sites are pretty interesting in their own right. St. Paul's or Westminster Abbey alone could keep you occupied for hours, so if you want to soak up the atmosphere in any of these special places, allow yourself plenty of time.

A church with a known history dating from before the reformation (1530s) is always a prime suspect for a ley mark point, particularly if it occupies a prominent hilltop position. St. Paul's Cathedral is a hilltop location dating from 604 or thereabouts and there has been speculation that it may have previously been the site of a temple dedicated to Diana Artemis and, even earlier, the site of a stone circle.

From its hilltop position on the crown of Ludgate Hill, it rightly dominates the London skyline, shaming the more modern architectural howlers that have been built around it.

So it should come as no surprise to find it features in our first ley, not to mention a few others later in the book.

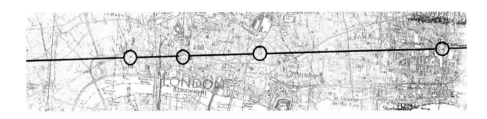

Illustration 1:
Alfred Watkins' St. Paul's Ley and its main mark points: The Temple Church,
St. Paul's Cathedral, St. Helen's Bishopsgate and St. Dunstan's Stepney.

Chapter Four

The St. Paul's Ley

Main mark points;
**1: The Temple Church. 2: St. Paul's Cathedral.
3: St. Helen's Bishopsgate. 4: St. Dunstan's Stepney.**

Other mark points;
**5: St. Mary's at South Ealing. 6: A holy well beneath The
Aldwych. 7: Site of Old Pol's Cross. 8: A length of old
straight road (Bulls Lane) in Stepney and 9: The church
yard of St. Mary Magdalene, East Ham.**

In **The Old Straight Track**, Alfred Watkins describes this ley
as follows:

*"The Temple, St. Paul's Cathedral and St. Helen's Bishops-
gate align to St. Dunstan's Stepney which has pre-Conquest remains,
while two other churches and the Bank site (where there was a
church) are on the ley. "*

Alfred Watkins took the Temple Church as his starting point and
does not mention any mark sites to the west of it.

I am not sure what scale map old Alf was using, but on modern
Ordnance Survey sheets, both 1:25,000 and 1:50,000 the alignment
goes very close to St. Clement Danes' Church by The Aldwych.

Using a very large scale street map for accuracy, I found the
alignment passes through the Aldwych, between St. Clement Danes and
St. Mary Le Strand. Much of this area was originally part of the church-

yard of St. Mary-le-Strand and while neither church is actually on the alignment, we can add one extra mark point. Old maps from the last century show a Holywell Street in this area and, I am told, the holy well is actually still there, accessible via a manhole in the basement of Australia House.

Judging by the position of this well on early Ordnance Survey maps, it could be definitely on Watkins' St. Paul's Ley.

As this well is sometimes confused with St. Clement's Well, I've reproduce here a snippet from **The Times** of **May 1st, 1874**, which indicates that St. Clement's Well was actually further east and to the north of St. Clement Danes' church, in the area now occupied by the Law Courts:

"The holy well of St. Clement, on the north of St. Clement Danes Church, has been filled in and covered over with earth and rubble, in order to form part of the foundation of the Law Courts of the future. It is said that penitents and pilgrims used to visit this well as early as the reign of Ethelred."

Watkins obviously thought the alignment did not extend any further west than The Temple Church. However, after the Aldwych Holy Well, it does seem to have a few near misses. The alignment passes through the south side of the churchyard of St. Anne's in Soho, near the junction of Wardour Street and Shaftesbury Avenue. It takes in the south side of the American Embassy in Grosvenor Square. Then it crosses Park Lane and runs through the north side of Hyde park passing a few yards north of the Peter Pan Statue and The Speke Monument in Kensington Gardens.

As it exits the park, it has a near miss with St. George's Church in Campden Hill, passing to the north of it, then heads off towards Holland Park tube station.

More distantly, it seems to align to the old St. Mary's Church next to The Rose and Crown at South Ealing.

Apart from the Holy Well and St. Mary's in South Ealing, there are really no other notable connections in that direction, so let's return to Watkins' starting point, the Temple Church, and investigate the alignment to the east.

The Temple Church

The Temple Church, of course, is one of Britain's few round churches and its shape was of paramount importance to the Templars. It takes, as its model, the round Church of the Holy Sepulchre in Jerusalem. As the supposed site of Christ's burial, the Templars were said to regard the Church of the Holy Sepulchre as the most sacred place in the world's most sacred city. To the Crusaders, every round church they built symbolically recreated the sanctity of this most holy place. It may be significant that it is dedicated to Mary, not Christ.

When the Temple church was designed, its axis was aligned directly to St. Paul's straight along the ley. The original huge double entrance doors at the western end of the circular nave open directly on the ley, which runs the length of the later rectangular extension along its central aisle and directly through the altar. There is a very good reason for this orientation to St. Paul's.

According to **Adrian Gilbert** in his book, **London The New Jerusalem**, the Temple Church is the same distance from St. Paul's as The Church of The Holy Sepulchre in Jerusalem is from the Dome of the Rock.

The Dome of the Rock, was, of course, the site of Solomon's Temple and the Knights Templars' first HQ in Jerusalem. As such it would have been greatly revered by them, possibly even more so than The Holy Sepulchre. From this, we can safely assume that the Templars somehow equated St. Paul's with this primary place of sanctity.

To mark its importance, the Temple Church was personally consecrated on Februay 10th, 1185, by no less a personage than Heraclius, the patriarch of The Church of The Holy Sepulchre in Jerusalem.

Heraclius had travelled all the way to London from The Holy Land specifically for the purpose. No easy journey in those days. A fact which confirms and emphasizes the importance of this place to the Templars. It was so revered, that only the most powerful, influential and important Templars could be buried here, for to be interred in the round church was as good as being buried in Jerusalem itself.

Allow yourself plenty of time on your visit to this wonderful old place. There are regular guided tours and much to see, including some spectacularly hideous heads that grimace at you from the circular walls.

If you can relax under such daunting surveillance, there are seats around the circular church where you can sit, marvel at the sacred geometry of the building and absorb the presence and power of the place.

When you leave, pay a visit to the nearby Fountain Court and sit quietly beneath its famous and gnarled old mulberry trees. On the way, look out for flying horses. Images of Pegasus abound in the Temple grounds. The winged white horse is the symbol of the Inner Temple.

From the Temple Church, the ley runs roughly parallel to Fleet Street and passes just to the south of St. Bride's Church, through the site of the Bridewell penitentiary and possibly the old Whitefriars' Priory, then alongside Pilgrim Street to Ludgate Hill and St. Pauls.

St. Paul's Cathedral

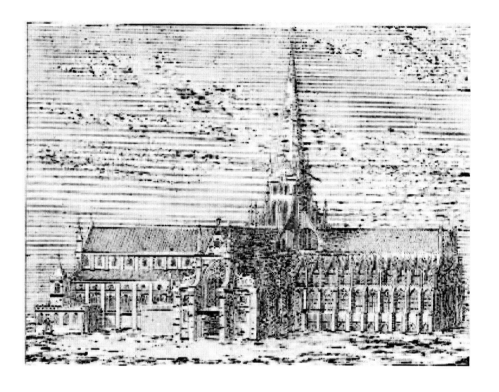

Illustration 2: Old St. Paul's

At St. Paul's, the ley is said to run directly along the north aisle of the Cathedral which was a church path prior to Wren's re-construction of the building. Whatever map you use, the ley certainly seems to run along the north side. What no-one seems to have commented on before is that there are a couple of curiosities close to the path of this ley.

The first is a strange altar-like stone hidden away behind a clump of bushes on the Cathedral's NE side, so the casual visitor would not even notice it. I'm no expert on these things, but I have been told that it resembles a small, plain Roman altar stone. Some people refer to it as the Diana Altar and consider it to have been evidence of the Temple to Diana Artemis which legend insists once stood upon this site. Better evidence actualy exists in the form of a more ornate Roman Diana Altar found during the construction of The Goldsmith's Hall (within walking distance of St. Paul's) and which used to be on display in the Court Room (it may still be).

Whatever this stone is, altar or not, it is directly on the ley and few visitors to the Cathedral notice it.

St. Paul's foundation as a sacred site is lost in the mists of time. It probably dates right back to the era of London's legendary founder, Brutus the Trojan, grandson of Aeneas, who was guided to Britain by a vision of the Goddess Diana Artemis.

Nennius, Geoffrey of Monmouth and other historians inform us that when Brutus arrived here and declared it his capital, he called it New Troy or Trinovantum and founded a temple of Diana in honour of the goddess whose vision had led him here. Ludgate Hill is considered by many to be the site of that temple. Hard evidence for its existence is scarce, though the Goldsmith's Hall's Diana Altar is hard to dismiss, as is the evidence in the records of the historian William Camden. According to the Aquarian Guide to Legendary London, he wrote:

"Some have imagined a temple of Diana stood here and their conjectures are not unsupported. The neighbouring old buildings are

called in the church records, Camera Dianae, and in the reign of Edward I were dug up in the churchyard an incredible number of oxheads which were held by the multitude with astonishment as the remains of heathen sacrifices and it is well known to the learned that Taurobolia were celebrated in honour of Diana. When I was a boy I have seen the head of a buck, fixed on a spear (which seems to agree with the sacrifices of Diana) carried about with great pomp and blowing of horns within the church...the custom certainly savours more of the worship of Diana and heathenism than Christianity."

Illustration 3: Was St. Paul's the location of a Temple of Diana ? This ornate Roman Altar to Diana was found during the construction of Goldsmith's Hall.

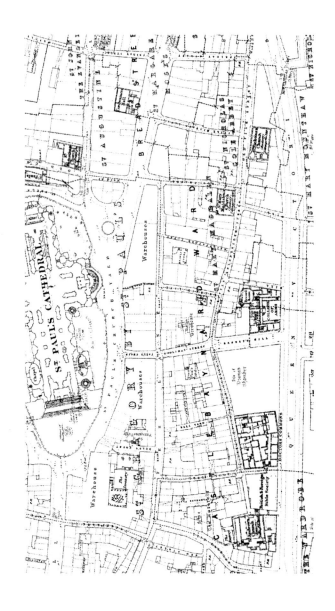

Illustration 4: An old map showing the site of the Chambers of Diana, to the south of the Cathedral.

The destruction of the Pagan temples at Ludgate Hill must have happened around 597 AD, when the Saxon King Aethelbert of Kent had the first St. Paul's built upon this sacred site of the Celtic Britons.

After Aethelbert and one of his subordinate Kings, Saeberht of Essex, both died in 616 AD, the people of London reverted back to Paganism, and Mellitus, The Bishop of London, who had been sent here by Pope Gregory on a mission to convert the Pagan Saxons, had to flee to Gaul. It was another fifty years before Christianity returned to the capital - meaning that London was essentially pagan up until the 7th century AD.

As well as the anomalous altar, at the North East end of the building is also the probable site of an old megalithic stone. Look carefully and you will find an octagonal shape on the ground indicating the original location of "Old Pol's Cross" "Or Old Pol's Stump" – an ancient stone into which the cross was set.

It later became an open-air pulpit. It was destroyed by Cromwell and replaced, only in the last century (and a few yards to the North West), by a huge monument and column topped by a gilded statue of St. Paul.

You can't miss it and, of course, it's nothing like the original Old Pol's Cross. That was not merely a monument. It marked the site of an open-air parliament and place of free speech much like the Stone of Free Speech upon Parliament Hill in Hampstead.

As such, its origins would be equally ancient.

Like so many other crosses, it may have been initially a standing stone of uncertain antiquity, later Christianised by the addition of a cross.

It was also, traditionally, a place where a King-to-be would face a public vote on his right to the crown, prior to his coronation.

Interestingly, in La Morte D'Arthur, Sir Thomas Mallory states specifically that Arthur won the right to be king by drawing a sword from a stone in the churchyard of the greatest church in London, obviously St. Paul's, so perhaps this was the stone.

As for its name, Old Pol, we are told, is a coloquial reference to St. Paul. I don't think so. That explanation is highly unlikely and is probably part of the Christianisation of this site whose tradition as a holy place pre-dates Christianity by a considerable period. Besides, why would St. Paul, be "Old" anything?

Old Pol suggests something far more ancient and is more likely to have been the old pagan sun god, Apollo, sometimes known as Helios Apollo, whose Saxon equivalent, Balder, was also known as Phol.

So if this was Old Pol's stone, it was probably associated with the sun, or sun god and therefore would be likely to have been the most important stone (or King Stone) of any megalithic monument here.

Similar stones, like the King Stone at The Rollright Stones and the "heel, hele or helios" stone at Stonehenge mark a midsummer sunrise alignment, so this one could have marked a significant sunrise from the stone circle that E.O. Gordon (author of **Prehistoric London,** 1925) claims once stood on Ludgate Hill.

In support of this argument, the stone or cross actually stands on a midsummer sunrise line through St. Paul's which is documented later in the book as the Coronation Line.

We'll never know for certain, but we can be sure that whatever stone marked the site of the original Old Pol's Cross, it stood on this important junction of leys upon the city's most important sacred hill.

When visiting this spot, you'll find several benches circling the original site of the stone and cross. Ideal for sitting quietly to pick up impressions of the place and to try to imagine what actually made it sacred before any cathedral was constructed here.

Will your inner vision reward you with a glimpse of an ancient stone circle, Brutus's New Troy, classical temples to Diana and Apollo, or an ancient druid oak grove ? Will you meet the druids here, as St. Paul himself was said to have?

Illustration 5: The original site of Old Pol's Cross, or Old Pol's Stump. Is this where King Arthur pulled his sword from the stone ?

Illustration 6: The more recent St. Paul's Cross.

St. Helen's Bishopsgate.

According to an old and threadbare booklet (one of many in my library) entitled **The London City Churches,** compiled by The London Society and priced at one shilling, a church may have occupied this site since before the Norman Conquest. It certainly has the atmosphere of a very ancient and sacred foundation and is believed to stand on the site of a pagan temple.

The first verifiable mention of the church is in 1161 in a grant of land made to the Priory of Southwark. Then, in 1210, The Dean and Chapter of St Paul's gave permission to establish a nunnery of the Benedictine Order in the grounds of the Priory Church of St Helen. The church's unique double nave stems from this combined foundation.

The unusual dedication supposedly relates to Helen, mother of Constantine, the first Christian Roman Emperor in the fourth century. Local legend claims that Constantine himself founded the church in memory of his mother, though most church guides predictably cast doubt on this suggestion. If there is any truth in it at all, it must be a very important spot and an extremely ancient sacred site.

Illustration 7: Great St. Helen's, Bishopsgate

An alternative suggestion is that back in those times, the name Elen was remembered (particularly in Wales) as the goddess and guardian of the old travellers' ways and by some folks nowadays, as a Goddess of the leys.

So for this most ancient of her shrines to appear on this alignment is possible confirmation that an ancient path or track ran through here. It is therefore no coincidence that the alignment of the ley runs directly along the axis of the church, as it did at the Temple church.

The atmosphere of the place is quite inspiring. My feeling is that this site is far older than its known history and that an ancient goddess was venerated here. Take time here to sit patiently and let her speak to you.

St. Dunstan's in Stepney

St. Dunstan's in Stepney also aligns directly to the ley and the Rocque map of 1746, shows a road opposite the church, called Bull Lane which the ley would have followed before entering St. Dunstan's. Had he noticed it, Watkins would have counted that as an additional mark point and possibly evidence of an old straight track. Shame how time erases these things.

St. Dunstan and All Saints church, in Stepney High Street (originally White Horse Lane), is a church of great antiquity, by far the oldest church in the borough. Records tell us that it dates from not long after Stibba, the Saxon warrior, who is thought to have given Stepney its name, first landed here. Chances are though, it may have been in use as a sacred place even earlier.

Dunstan, Bishop of London and Lord of the Manor of Stepney, replaced the small wooden church on this site with a new stone church dedicated to All Saints sometime around the year 952. When Dunstan was canonised in 1029, the name was changed to St. Dunstan and All Saints. Until the early 1300s, it was the only church for miles around, serving a large area east of the City of London.

The present church is the third one on the site and dates largely from the 1400s although the chancel, where the altar stands, is 200 years older and the font is over 1,000 years old.

The bells have a familiar ring to them, being commemorated in the old rhyme 'Oranges and Lemons:' "When will that be, say the bells of Stepney." The oldest of the ten bells was recast in 1385.

Despite all this recorded history, an old local told me that Stepney takes its name from The "Stepping Stones" which could once be found here. Stepping Stones Farm is certainly near the church, but what the "stepping stones" were is anyone's guess since they are no longer in evidence and there is no river or stream for any literal stepping stones to cross. Maybe they were Stibba's Stones?

I suppose that the site, like so many other sacred places, could have been marked in its remotest history, by a megalithic stone monument, now almost completely forgotten.

The only evidence I can offer for this is from a personal experience. On my first visit to the church, I saw, clairvoyantly, a white robed, druid-like figure standing beside the church entrance.

Next to him was a large stone, about four feet wide at its base and four feet high, tapering to a rounded point. He said it was The Dun Stone.

A similarly named stone near Widdecombe in Dartmoor was traditionally used as a location for collecting tithes.

If there ever was a Dun Stone at Stepney, it is long gone without trace, except in the etheric memory banks of the place and possibly my imagination.

The Parish Church of St. Mary Magdalene, East Ham.

On the 1;50,000 Ordnance Survey map, the St. Paul's Ley looks as if it might extend beyond St. Dunstan's. First, to a St. Paul's church in Burdett Way, which is not particularly ancient. Then, to the vicinity of St. Mary's churchyard in East Ham, which most definitely is.

The Parish Church of St. Mary Magdalene, East Ham, is a treasure. It is the oldest Norman church in London to have survived intact. Roman burials have been excavated nearby and the antiquarian William Stukeley chose to be buried in an unmarked grave somewhere within its churchyard, which is now bursting with life as a nature reserve.

St. Mary's is also a mark point of the Barking Triangle in the London Earthstars landscape temple geometry.

It is well worth a visit, especially on a summer's day and the interior of the church, if you are lucky enough to be allowed to see it, is spectacular, with very intense energy.

Illustration 8: The Parish Church of St. Mary Magdalene, East Ham.

38

Final thoughts.

This fresh look at Watkins' original investigation of the alignment has turned up some additional supportive evidence. It can now count five extra mark points in the form of St. Mary' s South Ealing, the Aldwych Holy Well, the mysterious Diana Altar, the site of Old Pol's Cross or stone and the alignment of the former Bulls Lane near St. Dunstans. Unfortunately, we can't count St. Mary's East Ham as an extra mark site, as the alignment does not go directly through the church, only its churchyard.

The fact that several churches are actually aligned to exactly the same orientation as the ley seems to indicate some relevance to the alignment and recognition of it in the past. However, the significance of the orientation is a mystery to me. The St. Paul's Ley runs four degrees north of east, very close to an equinox sunrise in the east and sunset in the west, but not particularly precise.

The Equinoxes, for those who don't know, occur twice a year when day and night are precisely equal. Usually, they fall around March 21st for the Spring Equinox and September 21st for the Autumn Equinox. By my calculations, 4 degrees north of east could relate to a sunrise and sunset about a week after the Spring Equinox or a week before the Autumn Equinox.

A week after the Spring Equinox would correspond to a date close to the end of March or beginning of April. If it relates to April Ist, All Fool's Day, perhaps a there was a celebration of the fool, the green man, the old god of nature, on this day, way back in the mists of time. Also, the Christian Holy Week which culminates in Christ's resurrection can occur around this time, so perhaps there is some hidden relevance there, too.

The September date would be around 13th and, as far as I can ascertain, isn't remarkable for anything relevant, unless our ancestors' equinox celebrations were spread over a whole week – which could be entirely likely.

Chapter Five

The Strand Ley

1: St. Martin's in the fields 2: St. Mary-le-Strand 3: St. Clement Danes 4: The site of the Temple Bar, the western gate of the city 5: St. Dunstan's-in-the-West Fleet Street 6: St. Sepulchre Snow Hill   7: St. Bartholomew-the-Less 8: The Mount, Arnold Circus, Shoreditch.

Additional mark points:
9: St. James' Palace 10: Green Park   11: The Gardens of Buckingham Palace 12: St. Columba's Church of Scotland in Pont Street 13: St. Mary-le-Boltons churchyard 14: St. Luke's, Redcliffe Gardens.

This is an excellent ley to walk, starting from St. James' Palace or St. Martin-in the-fields, which is no longer in open countryside, but in an extremely busy area, overlooking the concrete fields of Trafalgar Square.

As you stroll along The Strand, particularly near the Lyceum, you can see for yourself how well the church spires of St. Mary-le-Strand and St. Clement Danes line up ahead of you. You may also feel the energy of the ley at these points if you are sensitive to such things.

Watkins description of the ley in **The Old Straight Track** is surprisingly brief and includes an obscure reference to a book about the Romany Language which few will have ever heard of. Here's what he writes about it:

" St. Martin's in the fields. St. Mary-le-Strand, St. Clement Danes and St. Dunstan's Fleet Street, align to the site of an ancient mound (approximately at Arnold's Circus, Shoreditch) described by

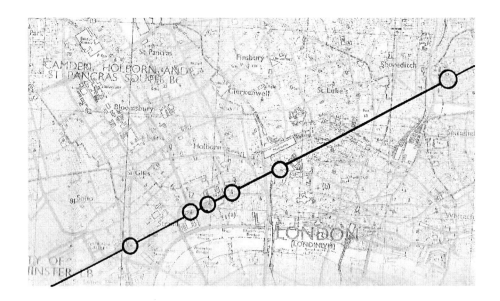

Illustration 9:
Watkin's Strand Ley. St. Martin's in the fields - St. Mary-le-Strand - St. Clement Danes - the site of the Temple Bar, the old western gate of the city - St. Dunstan's-in-the-West Fleet Street - St. Sepulchre Snow Hill - St. Bartholomew-the-Less - The Mount, Arnold Circus, Shoreditch.

Borrow in a chapter called "The Mount" in "Romano Lavo-Lil" and this is verified as a track by lying approximately on part of The Strand and Pall Mall."

In fact, the alignment also takes in a couple of other sites and places of interest, including the the Church of the Holy Sepulchre in Snow Hill. Obviously, not all of these places would have been considered valid mark points by Watkins but I think they are worth highlighting in order to give you a clearer picture of the possible course of the ley.

St. Martin's-in-the-fields

St. Martins, by contrast, is a perfect mark point. It has a known history as a place of worship for almost 800 years, the first church on this site being recorded in the year 1222. Actually, it could be a great deal older. A Roman coffin was found nearby dating from the fifth century and a dedication to St. Martin on a site of this antiquity is sometimes associated with a previous temple dedicated to the Roman God Mars. The present church is the third on the site and dates from the 18th century. During its construction, remains of a Roman brick arch were found, along with the bones of prehistoric animals and a human skeleton over eight feet tall. What became of these finds is not known.

On a more mystical note, the ley passes diagonally through the church (oddly the church is sited at the same orientation as the St. Paul's Ley rather than this one) and may be felt strongly in several places, including immediately in front of the main doors. This is directly above a round bell-shaped chamber in the crypt. Several people, including me, have felt unusual energy sensations when they have walked across the front of the building, exactly where the ley passes through. Some felt a tingling in their hands, others a sensation in their legs. At least one person has reported feeling suddenly unbalanced as if blown by a strong wind.

While you're looking around, don't ignore the new, painfully modern entrance to the crypt on the north side of the building. It leads to an impressive new gallery area and beyond that, to the atmospheric vaulted crypt, containing a very good café.

The Strand

From St. Martin's, the alignment follows part of The Strand. Watkins thought this verified the Ley as an old track, since Fleet Street and The Strand have formed the main artery to the west from the City of London since Roman times and probably before. From the 6th to 9th centuries, the area from The Strand to Covent Garden was the very heart of London's Saxon settlement, Lundenwic. The older Roman city of Londinium stood abandoned to the east.

The Strand (a Saxon word simply meaning foreshore) itself had been deemed by various princes and bishops, from Norman times to the Reformation, to be the perfect place to build a palace.

The road eventually became lined with them: a sort of early Bishop's Avenue or Millionaire's Row. The Bishops of Worcester, Llandaff, Coventry and Lichfield built impressive residences here as did Count Peter of Savoy, the uncle of Henry 111, who built the Palace of the Savoy in the 1240s.

At various places along the Strand, you can see clearly how well the churches line up or even feel the flow of the energy in the ley. If you do feel inclined to whip out your dowsing rods in the middle of The Strand, don't let it distract you from the lethal London traffic.

St Mary-le-Strand

The first record of a church here, dedicated to the Nativity of the Blessed Virgin Mary, dates from 1147 and its churchyard originally extended as far as the Waldorf Hotel at the Aldwych (or so an old sign in the church tells us). Thomas a Becket was once the rector of this church before being murdered at Canterbury in 1170.

The current building, despite being aligned directly to the course of the ley, does not stand on the site of the original church. That occupied a location now covered by Somerset House.

The old church was demolished in 1548 by Edward, Lord Protector who wanted a renaissance palace in what was then the most fashionable part of town and wasn't going to let a mere house of God stand in his way. Such was his perceived immunity from divine wrath and retribution, he also demolished the Priory of St. John at Clerkenwell and the chapter house of St. Paul's to provide masonry for his palace. It still stands as Somerset House and, as a result, for 175 years, there was no church here at all.

Although some way from its original site, today's church still stands within the original churchyard boundaries and has a very interesting history. It was the site of London's most famous maypole and the Strand Cross, possibly another important ancient stone which had been Christianised by the addition of a cross.

The Cross seems to have dated back at least to Norman times, but could have marked a site that was a great deal older since it must have been a place of some importance and reputation.

Records show that local magistrates held their assizes in front of it, in the 13th century. In the 17th century, the Strand Cross was replaced by a windmill used to pump water – suggesting a nearby well. Possibly the previously mentioned Holy Well, and in turn, the windmill was replaced by a maypole, obviously suggestive of a site of pagan celebrations.

This last association is interesting since the orientation of the Strand Ley is very close to a MayDay sunrise alignment and could have constituted a sighting line, in the days when you might have been able see the sun's rising point from this spot.

Cromwell didn't much like the pagan associations of the May -

pole (nor the fun probably) and ordered his killjoy puritans to demolish it. Not to be outdone, the locals replaced it with a new one in 1661. It survived until 1717, when it was removed and various remnants presented to Sir Isaac Newton re-built into the base for a telescope.

The current church was built around between 1712 and 1717, though not consecrated for use until 1723. It's an extravagant Baroque style designed by James Gibbs, who was the architect of St. Martin' s and who studied in Rome where he acquired the inspiration for many of St Mary-le-Strand's features.

This was his first public building and it won him considerable fame. The interior of the structure is richly decorated with a ceiling inspired by the churches of Santo Apostoli and the Santa Luca e Martina in Rome. The walls were influenced by Michaelangelo and the steeple shows the influence of Wren. In short, it is well worth a visit. Sadly, its current location, on a traffic island in the middle of a hectic one-way system, often prompts people to suggest its name should be changed to St. Mary-le-Stranded.

St. Clement Danes

Like St. Mary-le-Strand, St. Clement Danes occupies an island in the Aldwych one-way system and has a long history as a sacred site. They stand in such close proximity that they must have had some ancient common foundation in some larger and more ancient sacred enclosure, which surely included the nearby vast churchyard of St Mary-le-Strand and was probably centred on the life-giving sacred waters of the holy wells in this area.

The known origins of St. Clement Danes takes us back nearly a thousand years and other references suggest it may be even older. Records show that a stone church replaced a wooden one here in 1022. Some of the original stones are still in the base of the tower.

The association with Danes has three possible origins. One version tells

45

us that in 886, Alfred the Great allowed Danes who had married Eng -
lish women to settle in the area. However, Stowe writes that *"the
parish church of St. Clement Danes, is so called because Harold, a
Danish king, and other Danes were buried there."*

Going back even further, the site may have been a Roman
Cemetery and there is a well on the Eastern side which some consider
to have been the former St. Clement's Well. This seems unlikely in the
light of the article I found from the The Times of May 1st, 1874, which
clearly indicates that St. Clement's well was further to the north of St.
Clement Danes' church, and is now lost beneath the Law Courts.

So if there is a well beneath the eastern end of St. Clement
Danes, it's another one.

This is an impressive church, and one whose steeple can be seen
to line up with others along the ley. Its crypt provides interesting sensations from the ley and from underground water sources, as well as
being a good spot to spend some time soaking up the atmosphere of the
place.

Be warned that your peace may be shattered by the bells ringing
out the old 'oranges and lemons' nursery rhyme tune with which St.
Clements has long been associated. The main body of the building was
re-built by Wren, the spire added by Gibbs.

The site of Temple Bar

This marked one of the old gates into the City of London. It
stood in Fleet Street roughly mid-way between St. Clement Danes and
St. Dunstan's-in-the-West, adjacent to the Law Courts. A bar is
recorded at this location from as early as 1293 and was probably, at that
time, no more than some kind of wooden gate.

The surviving Temple Bar is an impressive design, reputedly
by Wren, and built in 1672 of Portland Stone. It is lucky to have

escaped the fate of the others gates, all of which were thoughtlessly de-molished. Temple Bar remained in position until 1878 when it was deemed an obstruction to horse-drawn traffic and was removed.

Sir Henry Meux, a brewer, acquired it as an entrance gate to his mansion at Theobald's Park, north of Enfield, where it remained for over a hundred and thirty years. It now serves as a pedestrian gateway to Paternoster Square, adjacent to St. Paul's.

Illustration 10: Temple Bar in the 1700s.

St. Dunstan's-in-the-West, Fleet Street

This is a wonderful church, which appears deceptively uninteresting if merely judged on its minimal neo-gothic frontage onto Fleet Street. Once inside though, you are treated to a rare octagonal nave which provides phenomenal resonance for singing or toning.

Like all the other churches on this alignment, its foundation is immeasurably ancient. There has probably been a church here since Saxon Times and the earliest recorded religious establishment dates from between 988 to 1070.

The current building was constructed in 1831 by John Shaw. If you are paying St. Dunstan's a visit, don't miss three things:

First, the only surviving statues of King Lud (who re-built Brutus's New Troy as Caer Lud from where London probably derives its name) and his sons Cassivellaunus and Nennius who stand in the church's courtyard doorway and who repelled Caesar's first attempts at an invasion of these isles.

Second, above them is a statue of Queen Elizabeth 1st dating from 1586, the only known statue to have been created in her own reign. It originally graced The Temple Bar.

Lastly, Gog and Magog, the giants who ring out the hours and the quarters on the bells of the church clock, which was the first public clock to have a minute hand.

For the more mystically inclined, the church provides a location for the junction of a number of leys, including a major Earthstars alignment (an axis of a huge five-point star) which runs from Bulstrode Camp at Gerrards Cross, through St. James at Gerrards Cross, St. Mary's at Denham, Horsenden Hill in Greenford and onwards via St. Bride's Fleet Street and the London Stone to Tower Hill. Try dowsing both lines and seeing if you can detect anything different between them.

It's worth noting that the Anglican Church now shares St. Dunstan's with the Orthodox Romanian Church, so if you turn up for a visit on a Sunday morning these days you will often find the air full of wonderful incense and the church packed to overflowing with Romanians.

Illustration 11:
Statues of King Lud and his sons Cassivellaunus and Nennius. These once stood on Temple Bar but are now hidden away in a side entrance to St. Dunstan's-in-the-West.

The Church of The Holy Sepulchre, Newgate, Snow Hill

On some maps, the alignment looks as if it passes slightly to the west of this church, explaining why Alfred Watkins and other ley hunters may not have noted it as part of The Strand Ley. The O.S. maps I am using warrant its inclusion.

The church itself stands on ancient foundations, records show a church was founded here as far back as 1137 and originally dedicated to St. Edmund.

It has Templar connections, too. This was an important setting off point for Crusaders and was re-dedicated to St. Sepulchre in the 15th Century.

One guide describes the building as *"an awe inspiring church with an interior like a cathedral."*

Having visited it on numerous occasions, I have to agree. Its exterior appearance hardly does justice to the atmosphere to be found inside. If you are passing, don't be tempted to walk on by without a visit. There is a presence and inspirational holiness here which cannot be explained simply by the architecture.

St. Bartholomew-the-less, Smithfield

St. Bartholomew-the-less is not to be confused with the far older St. Bartholomew-the-Great which stands some way to the north. The lesser Barts, stands within the hospital on the site of a mediaeval chapel, dating from the 15th century.

It is a spectacular octagonal structure designed by George Dance and like the other octagonal church on this line, St. Dunstan-in-the-West, it has wonderful accoustic resonance.

As a hospital chapel it is not marked on some maps, so other ley hunters may not have noticed that it's directly on this alignment.

The Mount, Arnold Circus, Shoreditch

The Ley Hunter's Guide states, as does Watkins, that the final mark point on the Strand Ley is the former site of a large mound called The Mount at Arnold Circus.

It is clear from this description that it is unlikely the authors ever visited the site because as soon as you do, you cannot help but notice that it is not the "former site of The Mount. A sizeable and unmistakable mound is still there.

It has been thoughtfully transformed into a circular traffic island in the middle of the junction and topped with an octagonal bandstand shelter.

I first stumbled upon this spot around 1990 when I was investigating another ley alignment, the Coronation Line. At that time the mound was a little neglected, but it had a remarkable atmosphere and almost magical presence.

Obviously I wasn't the only one to notice this as local residents banded together in 2004 to form the Friends of Arnold Circus and take care of this large piece of East End Heritage. They have lovingly tended the gardens, planted flowers and even had brass bands playing in the old bandstand, in order to bring the place back to life.

Sadly it seems a constant struggle against the local vandals. On my last visit (midsummer 2009) it looked as if someone had tried to burn the bandstand down.

Whether this is the original Mount or not is unclear. On at least one web site it is described as a burial mound dating from the time of the Black Death though I could find no other reference to this.

A fairly unlikely beginning, I would have thought, but you never know ....

The interesting thing is that the mound has several alignments directly aimed at it, not just the Strand Ley. As I mentioned earlier, The Coronation Line, one of London's most important alignments, also passes through the area of Arnold Circus, whilst a very long, arrow-straight stretch of Holloway Road is aimed directly at the mound.

If the name Holloway indicates an ancient Holy Way, the Holy Place to which is led was probably in the region of the mound at Arnold Circus – and for good reason – since it seems to have once been associated with a healing shrine and sanctuary of Mary.

Alfred Watkins' reference to it mentions an obscure book about the Romany language called **"Romano Lavo Lil"** and surprisingly, this tome throws quite a lot more light on the mound's sacred origins. Here's an excerpt:

" Not far from Shoreditch Church, and at a short distance from the street called Church Street, on the left hand, is a locality called Friars' Mount, but generally for shortness called The Mount.

It derives its name from a friary built upon a small hillock in the time of Popery, where a set of fellows lived in laziness and luxury on the offerings of foolish and superstitious people, who resorted thither to kiss and worship an ugly wooden image of the Virgin, said to be a first-rate stick at performing miraculous cures.

The neighbourhood, of course, soon became a resort for vagabonds of every description, for wherever friars are found rogues and thieves are sure to abound; and about Friars' Mount, highway-men, coiners, and Gypsies dwelt in safety under the protection of the ministers of the miraculous image.

The friary has long since disappeared, the Mount has been levelled, and the locality built over. The vice and villainy, however, which the friary called forth, still cling to the district.

It is one of the vilest dens of London, a grand resort for housebreakers, garotters, passers of bad money, and other disreputable people, though not for Gypsies; for however favourite a place it may have been for the Romany in the old time, it no longer finds much favour in their sight, from its not affording open spaces where they can pitch their tents. "

From this short piece we learn a lot. For a start, the Mount was associated with a nearby Friary and pre-dates *"the time of Popery"*. Presumably, that phrase refers to the era prior to Henry V111's self-motivated severence of England's ties with the Vatican and his dissolution and looting of the monasteries.

The Friary on a hillock could possibly be where the nearby St. Leonard's Parish Church originated, though the church history makes no mention of it.

Mounds sited near old churches are fairly common. Watkins' actually states that over forty churches in Herefordshire have mounds or moats adjacent to them. Usually they are of considerable antiquity and pre-date the church.

In fact, it is generally considered they were the centre of some ceremony or ritual activity before the churches came along and could be the reason why the churches were actually located there.

More importantly, we learn that a friary near to the Mount housed a venerated statue of The Virgin Mary, credited with miraculous healing powers. So this site was a renowned as a local healing shrine of some significance, despite the obvious cynicism of **Romano Lavo Lil**'s author.

This would explain perfectly why the old straight track of the Holloway Road points directly to The Mount. It was probably the Holy Way and main pilgrim's route leading to it.

Interestingly, a long straight tract of Ermine Street (now the A10) leads directly to the nearby St. Leonard's church, so the area is a crossing point of two very ancient routes.

The disappointing element in the extract from **Romano Lavo Lil** is the news that, at the time of the book's publication, the Mount had been levelled, which leads us to the inevitable conclusion that the mound in the traffic island may not be the original one, or at best, may only be its remains. Equally, it raises the question of why there is still a mound there at all.

My own theory is that the original Mount was considerably larger possibly on a scale with Merlin's Mount at Marlborough School and that the levelling process it underwent merely reduced its height to the twenty or so feet we see today.

To end on a positive note, whatever Arnold Circus' mound actually is, it is very definitely on an important node point and ley junction.

Yet another alignment to the mound comes through two of London's most important sites: the site of a former burial barrow on the side of Primrose Hill and the New River reservoir in Pentonville Road, which, prior to its thoughtless demolition by the Victorians, was the site of the Penton Pyramid, an ancient stepped mound mentioned in "**Prehistoric London**" by E.O. Gordon. The antiquity of these two mounds suggests a similar origin for the Mount in Shoreditch. Such a shame that all three have been "levelled".

If you visit the Arnold Circus Mound, you may find it is a place with a strange atmosphere. When I tried to "see" into the mound on my first visit, I received the impression of a very ancient gnarled and wisened old man with a mess of red hair, remarkably like the "bog burial" figure in the British Museum. I consider him to be a local Neolithic king or chieftan. Others have picked up imagery more in keeping with the plague pit theory. At the time of writing, I consider it to be a place that needs some care, attention and healing to lift its energy and improve the atmosphere.

Earthstars connections

On a 1;50,000 OS map, this alignment, like the previous one, can be extended to key points in the Earthstars Landscape Temple geometry around London.

To the west, the alignment leads directly to a mark site of the Earthstars' 30 point star: Strawberry Hill College near Twickenham. To the east, it passes close to St. Gabriel's church adjacent to Wanstead Flats - one of the points of the Earthstars pentagon (the other four points are St. Mary's East Barnet, Horsenden Hill Greenford, Caesar's Camp Wimbledon Common and Bellingham Green in South East London).

These points and the connections between them are an intrinsic part of the Earthstars' geometry and carry its characteristic energy and association with sites of healing and vision. Hardly surprising then to find this alignment is marked by several sites linked to holy wells or healing shrines.

Amongst them is a very important place of healing and vision: St. Bart's Hospital, where in 1123, Rahere, a courtier of Henry I, had a vision of Saint Bartholomew and consequently founded a priory and hospital at Smithfield on the site. The hospital and church still stand.

This particular alignment passes through the hospital's chapel dedicated to St. Bartholomew-the-Less, rather than the original church.

Yet like many of our great hospital chapels it is an impressive piece of architecture in its own right and adds another important place of healing and vision to this alignment.

Illustration 12:
The mysterious mound at Arnold Circus Shoreditch, standing at the crossing point of three leys, all of which are marked by sites of notable antiquity.

Chapter Six

Watkins' third London Ley,
The Temple Church and St. Bride's Ley
(The Piccadilly Line)

**1: St. Paul's Covent Garden 2: The Temple Church
3: St. Bride's Fleet Street 4: St. Martin's on Ludgate Hill
5: St. Vedast-alias-Foster 6: St. Lawrence Jewry near
the Guildhall 7: St. Stephen's Coleman Street
 8: St. Botolph's at Aldgate.**

In **The Old Straight Track**, Alfred Watkins listed this ley merely as line (b) on Page 124, with a brief description as follows:

"St. Paul's Covent Garden, The Temple, St. Bride's Fleet Street, a church on Ludgate Hill, one near the Guildhall, St. Stephen's, Coleman Street, all align to St. Botolph's Bishopsgate."

The authors of **The Ley Hunter's Guide**, Paul Devereux and Ian Thompson, point out that St. Paul's at Covent Garden isn't a pre-reformation church and therefore is not of sufficient antiquity to qualify as an accepted ley mark point. Nevertheless, it's a useful reference point for the course of the ley.

Personally, I don't regard leys as something exclusively related to our past. They have roots and history, of course, but I believe they also embody the living energies and life force of our planet and as such, are as relevant to the present and future as to antiquity and likely to be marked by all manner of appropriate buildings, ancient and modern.

I therefore present a few more questionable mark points for this alignment.

Illustration 13:
Watkin's Ley from the Temple Church through St. Bride's to St. Botolph Aldgate.

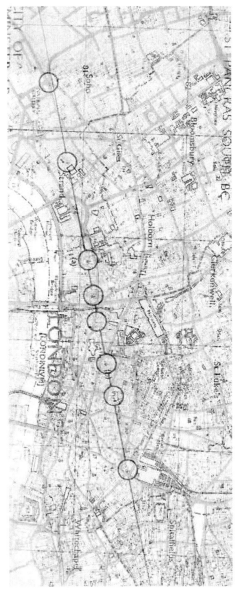

58

On a 1;50,000 O.S. map, it looks as if it passes through St. Mary-le-Strand, the present location of the Eros statue at Piccadilly Circus and directly through some of the ruins of Barking Abbey.

St. Mary-le-Strand turns out to be a doubtful mark point, since on larger scale maps, it's clear that the alignment goes to the west of the church, not through it. Nevertheless, this would definitely have been within the original churchyard boundaries.

Of course, Piccadilly Circus and the original site of Eros are not valid ley markers either, but it does serve as an interesting reference point for the westward course of the alignment which extends through Hyde Park, Kensington Gardens and Holland Park.

St. Vedast on the corner of Foster Lane to the NE of St. Paul's Cathedral is a questionable point. On some maps, it's on the line. With others, the alignment only clips the side of the church. It does, however, take in the church's small tranquil courtyard garden on its north side – an excellent spot to soak up the energy of the place, the ley and the Coronation Line which crosses it here.

A less uncertain mark point is Barking Abbey. This is around ten miles from central London and Watkins usually concerned himself with shorter leys, so he may not have bothered to extend his alignment this far.

Even so, on the 1:50,000 O.S. map, this ley definitely seems to extend to the ruins of the old Abbey. These lie some way to the north of the later St. Margaret's which is the church symbol shown on the map.

A clearly detectable energy ley can be dowsed running along the main axis of what used to be the abbey church, on roughly the same orientation as Watkins' ley.

Barking Abbey falls on at least one other ley in this book, but more importantly, it is one of the most significant points of The Earthstars Temple geometry around London.

That leaves us with the astonishing fact that all three of Alfred Watkins' original london leys, documented in **The Old Straight Track**, can be extended to major points in the Earthstars geometry.

Reference points for the extended Ley

Holland Park - Eros Statue at Piccadilly Circus - St. Paul's Covent Garden - The Temple Church - St. Bride's Fleet Street - St. Martin's within Ludgate - the site of a church called St. Michael's at Querne destroyed by the Great Fire of 1666 - St. Vedast's Foster Lane - St. Lawrence Jewry near the Guild Hall - site of St. Stephen's Coleman Street, destroyed by bombing in WW2 - St. Botolph's Without, Bishopsgate, near Liverpool St Station - Barking Abbey ruins.

Eros, Piccadilly Circus

Ah, we all recognise the winged figure with a bow and arrow, but is it Eros ? Apparently not.

It was designed originally to be the other Greek god of love, his brother Anteros and his statue commemorates the charitable works of Anthony Ashley Cooper, 7th Earl of Shaftesbury, hence it's official title, The Shaftesbury Memorial Fountain.

Eros (let's continue to call him Eros for the sake of familiarity) used to stand at the centre of Piccadilly Circus.

He now graces the pavement on the south east corner. The alignment seems to favour the old location rather than the new.

Whether someone sited the statue there consciously aware of the alignment is doubtful, but unconscious siting along leys does occur. As a symbol of love and charitable works, it is certainly a positive symbol to have as a focal point on any ley.

St. Paul's Covent Garden

Inigo Jones, well known architect of many a sacred plot, was also the creator of Covent Garden's Piazza and its adjoining St. Paul's church which was commissioned in 1631 by Francis Russell, Earl of Bedford and consecrated for divine worship in 1638.

It's a church with a split personality, since the main body of the building bears no resemblance to the neo-classical Palladian temple façade that graces the eastern side and provides an impromptu stage and backdrop for Covent Garden's wonderful barmy army of street entertainers.

By contrast, the church and quiet graveyard on the western side is a haven of tranquility and has the air of a secret garden, especially if approached through the darkened passageways from Henrietta Street or King Street.

Whichever side of the church you choose to seek inspiration and upliftment, you won't be disappointed.

The Temple Church

The Temple Church is where this ley crosses Watkins' St. Paul's Ley. The Angle of intersection is about 7 degrees, making the orientation of this ley about 11 degrees North of East.

More information about The Temple Church can be found in the section dealing with the St Pauls' Ley.

St. Brides Church Fleet Street

There is only one church dedicated to St. Bride in London and it is unique, for a variety of reasons. Firstly, for its antiquity as a sacred site. Its known history can be traced back to a Saxon church which stood here in the 6th century, though the presence of a well dedicated to

Bride or Bridget strongly suggests that it has been a shrine or place of sanctity for considerably longer and that the well was very probaby the original holy place.

Its second unique characteristic is that it is a perfect example of how successive cultures have utilized the same sacred sites over the course of many centuries.

When St. Bride's was rebuilt following its bombing during World War 2, the crypt revealed some long hidden archaeological secrets.

Beneath Wren's church had been a Norman structure.

Beneath that was a Saxon church with the stone coffin of a local King or Chieftain buried beneath the altar.

Below that was a mosaic floor of Roman origin.

Nowhere else exemplifies this sense of sacred site continuity quite as well as St. Bride's and, of course, it makes the place a very interesting spot to visit.

The crypt now houses a display of archaeological finds from the church as well as an exhibit relating to the local print industry which existed in this area for many years.

The well house, too, can be found in the crypt but is not open to the public. At the bottom of the crypt stairs is a long and sometimes spooky corridor lined with old stone coffin lids and other extraneous masonry. If you follow it to the end, you'll find a tiny square chapel with an altar, a few seats and an interesting atmosphere. The well house, I believe, is through a locked door on the other side of the chapel.

This, though, is a nice place to sit quietly and soak up the sense of presence and sanctity of the place.

Reputedly it dates from the 15th century and was a side chapel used by nuns, some of whom are still occasionally seen there.

I witnessed an apparition of a nun here some years ago. It was not a disturbing experience and has never been repeated. Presumably any wandering spirits of nuns here have now all gone about their heavenly business.

The main crypt entrance is on the right at the bottom of the stairs and is a large, light airy space considering its subterranean nature.

The stone coffin of the Saxon king and Roman flooring are easily found at the altar end and as several leys intersect at this point, one of them running directly along the axis of the church, the energy and atmosphere here can be interesting, sometimes vibrant, energizing and vital, at other times, bringing the tranquility that promotes introspection and inspiration.

In the past, St. Bride's well must have been held in some awe and connected to the sovereignty of the land.

Its water was traditionally sprinkled on the monarch's route to and from a coronation and, according to the references in the church crypt display cases, George 3rd used so much that the well ran dry and the tradition had to be discontinued.

There is much more which could be said about this wonderful old church. All the usual information about Wren and his wedding cake spire, you can glean from the church guide.

But for best results, sit yourself in the crypt and let the fabric of the building and the spirit of the place speak to you directly.

Illustration 14:
The crypt chapel next to the well house at St. Bride's Fleet Street. Since this photograph was taken, it has been re-decorated in a strangely modern style.

St. Martin within Ludgate, Ludgate Hill

This is Watkins' *"church on Ludgate Hill."* It's an inconspicuous spot. You could walk by St. Martin's and never notice it. Thousands do every day. There's no churchyard. Just a door from the street.

It's also a door into the mythic past, because this church stands on immensely ancient foundations. A plaque at the front of the church reads *" Cadwalladr, King of the Britons, is said to have been buried here in 677AD."*

So there was a church on this spot long before the mediaeval records which date from less than a thousand years ago, around 1174.

Legend has it that Cadwalladr had his ashes contained within an image of himself mounted upon a brazen horse, which was buried in a secret crypt beneath the church. The hidden crypt has never been found, but if it exists, Cadawalladr may not be alone in it. The legendary King Lud, who pre-dates Cadwalladr by over 700 years, was also reputedly buried here and gave his name to Ludgate, the original western entrance to his city, Caer-Lud, later to become London.

In mediaeval times, St. Martins Church actually stood up against the city walls, right next to the Ludgate which Geoffrey of Monmouth tells us, was erected by King Lud in 66 B.C.

When rebuilt by Wren between 1677 and 1684, the church was re-sited a few yards westwards to accommodate the widening of the road up Ludgate Hill.

According to various sources, it is used by some of the city's Masonic lodges and guilds and in 1962, became The Chapel of the Honorable Society of Knights of the Round Table. Funny, you never see their horses tied up outside.

Several alignments cross here, including the London Stone Ley and it feels very much like a solar energy site, though that may be more to do with Ludgate Hill itself, since Lud, mythologically, is synonymous with the ancient Celtic sun god Lugh.

St. Michael's at Querne

This church once stood on Watkins' alignment somewhere to the north east of Paternoster Row. Sadly it was one of the 86 churches destroyed by the Great Fire in 1666 and was never re-built. It's "at Querne" dedication relates to an 11th century reference which means it is "near a place where corn is sold".

St. Vedast-alias Foster, Foster Lane

For some reason, Watkins didn't notice this church was on the line. No-one knows why, but like St. Martin's on Ludgate Hill, it blends in a little too well with its surroundings from street level and could easily be missed. Nevertheless it's yet another City church that stands on an ancient foundation.

A place of worship is known to have existed here since the 12th Century and the unusual dedication to St Vedast relates to a sixth century saint, also known as St. Waast or Vaast on the continent, but as Vedast or Foster in England. Only three churches are dedicated to him in the whole country.

Inside, the church is typical of Wren, but with the pews neatly facing the aisle instead of the altar.

On the church's northern side is a secluded and tranquil square courtyard with paving laid out in a St. Andrew's cross whose SW – NE diagonal almost corresponds exactly with the axis of the Coronation L ine which also passes through the site.

St. Lawrence Jewry

This is only referred to by Watkins as a church near the Guildhall and unlike the last two on the alignment, it can hardly be missed.

It proudly dominates the south side of Guildhall Yard. It owes its name to the fact that the area was once a Jewish Quarter known as Old Jewry, but a Christian church has stood here since 1136.

Whether an earlier place of worship existed here is unknown, however it does stand above the site of a huge Roman amphitheatre, reputedly the largest in Britain, which once covered an extensive area now occupied by the Guildhall and yard.

Sadly, St. Lawrence's death was as gory as any of the goings-on in the amphitheatre. He was roasted alive by the Romans in 258 and subsequently attained the status of martyr. To commemorate this grisly end, the church's weather vane is in the shape of a gridiron.

The present building is yet another built by Wren (he must have been run off his feet). He completed this one between 1670 and 1687. It is a Guild church rather than a Parish church and is the official Church of the Lord Mayor and Corporation of London. The east wall is particularly special. Its stone facade is styled on a classical temple and has a pediment resting on four Corinthian columns. Inside, the white and gold interior is spectacular.

St. Stephens, Coleman Street

In Watkins' day, St. Stephen's Church still stood near the corner of Coleman Street and Gresham Street. Its history stretched back as far as the 13th century and, though it was destroyed by the Great Fire, it was rebuilt and survived until 1940 when German bombs finally flattened it, this time for good.

St. Botolph's without Bishopsgate

Here we have yet another sacred site of immense antiquity. The present church is the fourth on the site and was completed by James Gould under the supervision of George Dance the Elder in 1725.

During construction, the foundations of the original Saxon Church were discovered along with finds that suggest the strong possibility that worship on this site may have had Roman origins.

The earliest mention of the church dates from 1212 when it was referred to as 'Sancti Botolfi Extra Bishopesgate'. St. Botolph was a patron saint of travellers and there are three other St. Botolph's churches in close proximity to some of the city's other gates, presumably to allow travellers to ask for his blessing on their journey as they left the city – or to give thanks for a safe journey on their arrival.

Final thoughts

So at the final count, Watkin's third ley now has at least eight mark points of considerable antiquity, including a couple of truly unique spots to visit.

It's a good ley to walk and, depending on how long you linger at the sites, could take anywhere from two to four hours. Start at St. Botolph's in The City and finish in The Piazza at Covent Garden where you can rest your legs, enjoy a drink and snack and marvel at the lively buzz, good atmosphere and street entertainers. On the way, you'll have crossed a number of other leys and seen plenty of interesting sights.

The ley's distant connection to Barking Abbey merits a separate visit. Back in the 7th century, Barking was more important, grander and richer than Westminster Abbey. Very little of it still stands. Just a gatehouse and the foundations, set into the turf, as a mere groundplan of where the great walls once stood. Even the ruins are impressive. For dowsers, its a good site to practice. You can follow the leys through the walls instead of having to find a door.

As well as this ley, Barking Abbey falls on at least one other, the Stonehenge Line, one of London's most important alignments. But more importantly, it is an extremely significant point in The Earthstars Temple geometry around London. In fact, it's part of a triangle of local sites which which form the eastern gate of the city.

That means that all four of Watkins' original London leys documented in **The Old Straight Track**, (including the one in the next chapter), can be extended to major points in the Earthstars geometry.

That's an astonishing fact.

Is that a coincidence ? Or is it an indication that these simple ley alignments are part of a wider matrix of patterns on the landscape and in the life-force of the planet and are therefore best judged from the perspective of a bigger picture, rather than individually.

Illustration15: St. Vedast, Foster Lane, almost lost between the modern blocks.

Chapter Seven

Watkins' fourth Ley

St. George's-in-the-East - The White Tower - Southwark Cathedral - possible site of the Tothill Mound

The fourth London Ley in **The Old Straight Track** doesn't get much of a mention. It is almost as if Watkins himself was unsure of its validity, possibly because he only gives three definite mark points: St. George's-in-the-East, The White Tower at The Tower of London and Southwark Cathedral. Three sites would not have been considered a proveable ley, by the parameters he was setting at the time.

The fourth site which would give it more credence as a distinct alignment was in some doubt, and still is: The Tothill Mound, a man-made stepped pyramid which once stood somewhere in the Westminster area and whose location has been the cause of much speculation.

Watkins suspected that this alignment may pinpoint the location of the lost Tot-Hill mound. Here's what he says on page 133:

"Another orientation fact was revealed in plotting out a line from the White Mount (Tower) to Southwark Cathedral, which also goes through St. George's in the East. This alignment goes to West-minster and converges with a line down the middle of Tothill Street, to a point in Wellington Barracks.

Lines on the exact orientation of Westminster Abbey and the adjacent St. Margaret's Church were then laid down and converge to the above point.

Here then are four indications (one of them Tothill Street) of

convergence or orientation to one point, and it leaves a strong pre-
sumption that this was the point at which was situated the tot, toot or
mound, which gave its name to Tothill Fields and Street."

This had me confused at first, mainly because I took his mention of Westminster as a reference to the Abbey and the alignment does
not pass through the Abbey, it goes a good way North of it.

Once I realised that he simply meant Westminster in general,
everything dropped into place.

On a large scale street map, you can follow his reasoning. Lines
drawn along the axes of Westminster Abbey and Tothill Street do converge in the grounds on Wellington Barracks and could possibly indicate the site of the Tothill stepped pyramid mound.

Unfortunately, on the maps I used (1:10,000 approx) the axis of
St. Margaret's Church does not align to the same spot. I think Watkins
had even larger scale maps, so the difference may simply be down to
map inaccuracy. I hesitate to guess.

More recently, other researchers have expressed the opinion that
the Tothill Mound stood at a bend in the Horseferry road, a considerable distance from Tothill Street. One web site even claims it appears
on the 1746 map of London by Rocques, at this location.

My copy certainly shows Tothill Fields in that area, but as far as
I can see, no mound. Maybe I need better specs or a better copy of the
map. As the alignment does not seem to indicate any other noteworthy
sites and old Alf is no longer around to defend his corner, it doesn't
seem worth making too much of a fuss about.

What is worth further examination is another alignment that includes some of these sites, and a whole lot more, which I discovered
when I was plotting part of the Earthstars geometry.

Chapter Eight

The Stonehenge Line

1: Barking Abbey 2: Bow Common Church 3: St. George's-in-the-East 4: The Royal Mint 5: The Earthstars junction point on Tower Hill 6: The Tower of London 6: Southwark Cathedral 7: Palace of Westminster 8: Westminster Abbey 9: St. Mary's R.C. Church in Cadogan Street 9: St. Mary Le Boltons 10: Feltham 11: Staines 12: Caesar's Camp near Bracknell 13: Wick Hill 14: Stonehenge

As you can see, this alignment passes through a couple of sites shared with Watkins' fourth ley, though at a different angulation. The Tower of London and Southwark Cathedral are both large enough to allow plenty of leeway for different leys.

Unlike Watkins short alignment, this one has plenty of mark points and seems to extend over a considerable distance.

It takes in an extraordinary number of London's most well known sacred sites and tourist attractions: Barking Abbey, the Tower of London, Westminster Abbey, Southwark Cathedral.

More important, it creates a direct link through them to Britain's most significant ancient sacred site, Stonehenge.

In the oppposite direction, it passes through Hornchurch, Runwell and possibly Colchester.

So this just has to be one of the most important leys through the capital.

Here are the details of its individual mark points:

Illustration 16:
The Stonehenge Line. One of London's most important and
powerful leys.

Illustrations 17 & 18: The deceptive "ISIS" stone at Southwark Cathedral and the statue of the "Hunter God" rescued from the cathedral's well. This is possibly the Romano-Celtic deity Nodens.

Illustrations 19 & 20:
Above, the Earthstars' pentagonal junction point at Tower Hill.
Below, the western entrance to Westminster Abbey.

Barking Abbey

Barking Abbey is one of the treasures of East London, the senior convent of all England, and as worthy of a pilgrimage as Glastonbury, Bury St. Edmunds or Canterbury.

According to the Venerable Bede, the Abbey was founded by St. Erkenwald in AD 666 for his sister St Ethelburga. Bede recorded it thus:

"When Sebbi... ruled the East Saxons, Theodore (then Archbishop of Canterbury) appointed over them Earconwald to be their bishop in the city of London... before he was made bishop (he) builded 2 goodly monasteries, one for himself (at Chertsey in Surrey), the other for his sister Ethelburga... in the province of the East Saxons at the place that is named in Bericingum..."

The new monastery, dedicated to St. Mary, rapidly grew in wealth and influence until it was destroyed by the Vikings in 870. All that remains of the first Barking Abbey is a broken Saxon Cross.

Like the phoenix, Barking Abbey rose from its ashes to become even greater than before. By the time of the Domesday survey in 1086, the Abbey's possessions were widespread and extensive. It became the only early Saxon monastic foundation in Essex to survive until the Dissolution, probably as a result of its royal connections, which allowed the King to nominate each new Abbess on the death of the old, so queens, princesses and other relatives were successively awarded the position.

Barking Abbey was far more important than Westminster and the Abbess of Barking enjoyed precedence over all other abbesses, ranking as a baron.

In 1541 the Abbey was dissolved by order of King Henry VIII.

Illustration 21:
Some of the remains of Barking Abbey, one of the treasures of East London.

The nuns were pensioned off and the buildings demolished. For almost 400 years the abbey site was used as a quarry and a farm.

All that remains of the old abbey buildings are the foundations and the Curfew Tower or Fire Bell Gate (rebuilt about 1460).

Yet almost 500 years after its destruction, any pilgrim will find it is still fully functional as a centre of enlightenment and inspiration.

Anywhere that has been a place of devotion for as long as Barking Abbey generates an atmosphere of sanctity which remains long after the buildings have disappeared.

At Barking, you can stand amid the ruined walls and still sense the sacred architecture around you.

You can sense the spirit of the place, a beneficent Marian presence or "White Lady" over-lighting it.

Some have even glimpsed her as a more human scale figure amid the ruins. Or perhaps they were seeing an image of one of the nuns imprinted as a memory in the atmosphere of the place.

For dowsers, there's the added benefit of having no walls to get in the way. Just follow the energy lines wherever they take you.

This one runs about 10 degrees north of east. Watkins' Temple Church to St. Bride's Ley runs about 5 degree north of east.

St. Paul's Church, Bow Common

The original church here was destroyed by the Luftwaffe in the 2nd World War and I am not sure how old it was.

It has been rebuilt, but not in any classical style. It's modern, or it was in 1960 when it was consecrated. **The Architectural Review** has described it as; *"the most important church built in the 20th Century."* I have to say that's debatable. On first appearances, I didn't like the look of it. But appearances can be deceptive and there is much in the atmosphere of the place to recommend it.

The first thing to strike any visitor is the entrance.

It has spectacular inscriptions carved by Ralph Beyer, (who also created the inscriptions for the Tablets of the Word at Coventry Cathedral). They read: *TRULY THIS IS NONE OTHER – BUT THE HOUSE OF GOD – THIS IS THE GATE OF HEAVEN.*

This has been absorbed into the local culture, so getting here would be no problem. You simply ask the bus driver or taxi to drop you at the Gate of Heaven.

Other fascinating features are the mosaic angels which grace the four interior walls between triangular arches. They are the work of Charles Lutyens, grandson of the architect, Edwin Lutyens.

The mystically inclined will be interested to hear that in each corner of the church, is a representation of one of the four alchemical elements; earth, air, fire and water.

Take a visit and judge for yourself. At least then you'll be able to tell your friends you've been to the Gates of Heaven and back.

St George's-in-the-East

You'll find St. George's on Cannon Street Road, between The Highway and Cable Street. It's a large and elegant Church built by Wren's apprentice, Nicholas Hawksmoor, in the early 18th century.

It is frequently claimed that "Old Nick " Hawksmoor's churches form a sinister pentagram on the London landscape. This often repeated nonsense seems to stem from a 70s comic book story by Iain Sinclair called Lud Heat and was spread further by the plot of a Johnny Depp film about Jack The Ripper, luridly titled "From Hell."

Suffice to say, the idea is as much a work of fiction as the comic or the film. Hawskmoor only built six churches and by no stretch of the imagination do any of them link up to form a perfect pentagram.

Besides, Hawksmoor could not be held responsible for whatever pattern their locations might form because he did not choose the sites personally. St. Alphage in Greenwich, for instance, had already been a place of worship for over a thousand years when he rebuilt it.

Meanwhile, back at St. George's ....

As a post reformation church, Watkins would not have considered it old enough to be a valid mark site, particularly as there's little evidence to indicate an earlier sacred site. So that's another reason why he may have doubted his fourth London ley.

Nevertheless, more than one alignment passes through here and it is an impressive church, inside and out, with quite a strong atmosphere, energy and presence.

When the church itself is locked, you'll find that St. George's Gardens (the original burial ground) behind it, make a good spot to soak up the atmosphere of the place or dowse the energy flows through.

The Royal Mint

The London Mint is an ancient institution not connected to spiritual matters, unless, like many in the city these days, your only god is money. The Mint first came into existence in 886, during the reign of Alfred the Great, but was only one of many throughout the kingdom.

It moved to the Tower of London in 1279 and remained there the next 500 years, eventually acquiring a total monopoly in production of 'the coin of the realm' in the 16th century.

My personal feeling is that this alignment and the Coronation Line we feature later, include many sites with definite connections to the sovereignty and power of the land. In that context, the Mint also qualifies as a place of some power and influence.

Tower Hill and the Earthstars pentagonal junction point.

The next mark point on this alignment is on Tower Hill, overlooking both Tower Hill Gardens and the Tower itself. The exact location is on a grass verge between Tower Gardens and the road junction.

It's not a church but, as a hilltop, may have been an ancient ceremonial location. It also marks a junction point of a primary pentagonal pattern in the London Earthstars Geometry.

For many years, it was identified by a small black stone marker, engraved with the Broad Arrow symbol of British Royalty (three lines creating the impression of an arrow head, similar to the druidic awen symbol).

I believe this was one of the Tower's original boundary markers used in the annual "Beating of the Bounds" ceremony, but when I passed this way in 2008, I found that the stone had disappeared. At the time of writing (2010) it had not yet been replaced.

This junction point is a powerful energy centre in its own right. Through the Earthstars' pentagonal pattern, it connects directly to several important alignments and many sacred sites. Here are a few of them: The London Stone, St. Bride's Fleet Street, St. Dunstan's-in-the-West, One Tree Hill Alperton, Horsenden Hill Greenford, Platts' Hill, St. Mary's Church Denham, St. James' Church Gerrards Cross, Bulstrode Camp Gerrard's Cross, St. Mary's East Barnet, Alexandra Palace Hill, St. Gabriel's Wanstead Flats, Caesar's Camp Wimbledon Common, St. Georges' Nine Elms ,… and many more.

Traffic passing this spot is very heavy and a huge distraction if you want to try to attune to the spirit of place here. The energy lines are wide enough for you to find a park bench in Tower Gardens a few yards away where you'll be a little more sheltered from the noise.

The Tower of London

Most guide books tell us that The Tower of London was built by William The Conqueror and imply there was nothing on the site prior to his arrival. In fact, it was a one of the most important ritual sites in Britain long before William came along.

He built the White Tower, yes. And it is probably the best preserved Norman Building of its type in Britain. But it was built upon a previous site of great significance.

E.O. Gordon in her book, **Prehistoric London**, tells us that this was the location of The Bryn Gwyn, The White Mount, a chalk-faced ceremonial mound similar to Silbury Hill near Avebury.

Beneath it, or so legend tells us, lay the Head of Bran the Blessed which had been carried all the way from the druid stronghold of Anglesey to be buried here as a guardian of the British Isles.

The cult of the oracular head is typical of the Celtic tribes and so the origins of this tale could date back over a couple of thousand years or more before the Norman era.

Even today, the myth is remembered and heeded in the legend of the Towers' ravens (raven in Welsh is Bran). Their wings are kept clipped because, folklore says, if they ever leave the Tower, Britain will fall.

Clearly, this was a site of immense importance to the ancient Britons, a place of power linked to the destiny of these islands and the sovereignty of the land. No wonder one of William's first acts was to take over the site and build his castle here.

The White Mount, like Silbury Hill near Avebury, would have been originally faced with chalk. It would glow with reflected light, in the sunlight or moonlight, day and night, identifying itself as a place of natural power. Even today, that sense of being in a numinous place is apparent. This is one of Britain's pre-eminent power centres, ranking alongside Stonehenge to which it is connected by this alignment.

Many similar mounds, remains of the local power centres, still exist around our countryside. Most are still classified as the remains of Norman Motte and Bailey Castles, since the opportunistic Normans made good use of what was already there.

Others virtually identical, had their own irreplaceable legends, like Merlin's Mount in the grounds of Marlborough School which claims to be the burial place of Merlin. Or nearby Silbury Hill, which is the largest man-made mound in Europe and reputed to hold the remains of a mythical King Sil wearing gold armour and mounted on his white horse.

The alignment here is not directly through the White Tower. It cuts across the NW of the Tower's grounds, through the moat that marks the perimeter of the ancient sanctuary.

Southwark Cathedral

Next spot on the line is London's oldest Gothic church, otherwise known as Southwark Cathedral, or the Cathedral Church of St. Saviour and St. Mary Overie (apparently, that simply means Mary over the river).

Hidden away amongst the offices on the south side of London Bridge, it is often overlooked, yet is one of the most atmospheric of our Cathedrals.

The first conclusive proof of a church here comes in the Domesday Book of 1086 which records that a "monasterium" was present during the reign of Edward the Confessor (1042 - 1066) and had its own wharf *"for the profitable unloading of goods brought up the river"*.

Christopher Winn's book on London suggests that a nunnery was founded here as early as the 7th century. He also states that a well was discovered beneath the choir in 1971 and in it was found a statue of a Pagan hunting God, believed to have been put there in the fourth century. The statue is now on display near the refectory and could be a rare image of Nodens, who is related to Gwynn Ap Nudd who leads The Wild Hunt and sleeps beneath Glastonbury Tor.

Of course, the mention of a well, raises the usual question of whether the original focus of reverence here was actually the life-giving waters of the well. If so, the site could be immeasurably older than known records.

The place has a definite feeling of a divine feminine presence. It may even have been home, in pre-christian times, to a temple of Isis. A shard of Roman pottery has been found here bearing a Latin inscription which translates as; *"The Temple of Isis in London"*

When I first heard this, I visited Southwark, intending to see if

I could psychically pick up any impressions that might confirm an Isis connection here.

The first thing I noticed in the half light of the evening, was a gravestone near the western end of the Cathedral grounds which seemed to have ISIS carved upon it. On closer inspection it turned out to actually be a date, 1818, but it was a strange synchronicity.

Later I took a group there to do the same thing and many people picked up other interestingly appropriate impressions.

For those looking for somewhere to meditate or just relax and feel the atmosphere here, there are numerous pleasant spots inside and outside the church, not to mention an refectory serving excellent breakfast or lunch for a reasonable price and in delightful surroundings.

The Palace of Westminster (Houses of Parliament)

Originally, this was not the publicly subsidised social club of our pompous parasitic elite, it was the site of a Royal Palace, built by Edward The Confessor in about 1050.

It was occupied by successive sovereigns, until Henry VIII decided he was moving down the road to Whitehall.

Its use as a seat of government dates back to when the Palace's St. Stephen's Chapel, built by Henry III, was for centuries the meeting place of the Commons. St. Stephen's Hall now occupies the site, but beneath it, the original crypt chapel dedicated to St. Mary still remains.

The Stonehenge Line passes through the building. I am not sure if this is through the site of the crypt chapel, or not.

Like other sites on this line, it is an important place of temporal and spiritual power linked to the sovereignty and power of Britain.

Westminster Abbey

The Abbey at Westminster is built upon what was probably one of the sacred islands of the Thames - Thorney Island - at one time flanked on the north and south by two channels of the Tyburn River, which flowed into the Thames roughly where Downing Street and Great College Street now exist.

E.O. Gordon's **Prehistoric London** suggests this as the site of a stone circle but predictably and regrettably, there is not a shred of hard evidence for the claim, as far as I know. The book offers no clue as to where the idea originates, though as certain elements in the book make it clear that the author is herself a member of The Ancient Druid Order, we can hesitate a guess that it came from their records.

She also suggests it was the site of a temple dedicated to Apollo and destroyed by earthquake in the 5th Century. A thousand years later, the tradition seems to have survived. John Flete, the fifteenth century monk and historian, wrote that:

" London worships Diana and the suburbs of Thorney offer incense to Apollo."

The actual date of the foundation of the Abbey is uncertain. I am assured that it was not mentioned by the Venerable Bede who was around until 736, but tradition reliably ascribes it to the Saxon King, Sebert, who also founded St. Paul's, sometime around 604 to 610. The infinitely knowledgable John Michell in his **Guide to Sacred England**, quotes an even earlier foundation by King Lucius, in the second century.

The Abbey is said to be a place of vision. Legend has it that a fisherman witnessed a vision of St. Peter himself descending from heaven to personally and miraculously consecrate the building. This is usually dismissed as an invention of the monks in the thirteenth century. Men of God accused of God fibbing ? Whatever next ?

Edward the Confessor is popularly regarded as the founder of the modern Abbey though the current building is largely the work of Henry III.

It is linked to British Royalty as a place of Coronation and place of burial. Many of Britain's Kings and Queens chose this as their final resting place, as did so many other notable characters, that they succeeded in making it the most impressive necropolis in the country, with more funereal monuments and tombs than any other church.

There's actually so much to see, you could spend all afternoon here. Edward's tomb, the Coronation Throne (now without the Stone of Scone beneath it) and the small side chapels nearby are particularly atmospheric. One has a wonderful statue of the Madonna and Child. See if you feel anything from it.

As for tracking the alignment, it appears to enter the Abbey on the North side, roughly near the transept, and exits near the SW tower.

Finally, one place not to be missed is the octagonal Chapter House. If no-one's around, sound a good OM or sing your heart out. The place rings like a bell.

St. Mary's R.C. Church Cadogan Street

As far as I know, this isn't an ancient site (unless you are a teenager, then anything over twenty years old is ancient).

It's part of the Kensington & Chelsea Deanery, founded in 1798. The original church here was built in 1811, reconstructed in 1879 and consecrated on June 12th 1882.

Nevertheless, it has the atmosphere of a much-loved and used spiritual sanctuary which gives the impression of a foundation considerably older.

Illustration 22:
The Palace of Westminster. The towers of Wesminster Abbey's west entrance, visible in the background, were the work of Nicholas Hawksmoor.

St. Mary-le-Boltons

St. Mary-le-Boltons has the feeling of a quiet country church, probably because at its inception, it was.

The church dates only from 1850 when much of this area was open fields and farmland.

Yet like St. Mary's at Cadogan Street, it feels much older and its vesica-shaped churchyard could easily be imagined as the former site of some sacred enclosure.

Still, there must have been some good reason why its architect chose this particular spot and I would love to know what it was.

Those Victorians knew a thing or two about the correct placement and construction of sacred buildings. That much is obvious from the style and location of the many Parish Churches we've inherited from them.

Chapter Nine

The Most Important Ley in London

The Coronation Line

Mark sites

1: St. George's Hill, Weybridge, formerly a hill fort
2: Whiteley's Village, Weybridge
3: Waynflete's Tower and Moat, Esher - strictly private, no
   public access
4: All Saint's church, Kingston upon Thames - the original
   site of The King Stone from which the town may take its
   name
5: Putney Heath
6: The Peace Pagoda and golden Bhudda in Battersea Park
7: St. Stephen's Church in Rochester Row SWI
8: St. Matthews' Church, Great Peter Street
9: Westminster Abbey
10: St. Margaret's Westminster
11: Big Ben, clocktower of The Houses of Parliament
12: The Oxo Tower on the South Bank
13: Site of the Blackfriar's Monastery
14: St. Andrew's-by-the-Wardrobe
15: St. Paul's Cathedral
16: Site of Old Pol's Stump/Cross
17: St. Vedast alias Foster, Foster Lane
18: St. Mary Aldermanbury, remains and garden, Love
    Lane
19: Moorgate Station
20: The Chapel of The Open Book, Wilson Street
21: The site of the Priory of St. John Holywell at Shoreditch

Coronation Line mark sites continued

22: The Mount Arnold Circus
23: St. Matthew's Church, Bethnal Green
24: The probable site of the Leyton Stone
25: Hilltop and crossroads, beside the
Maypole pub, Chigwell Row, Essex.

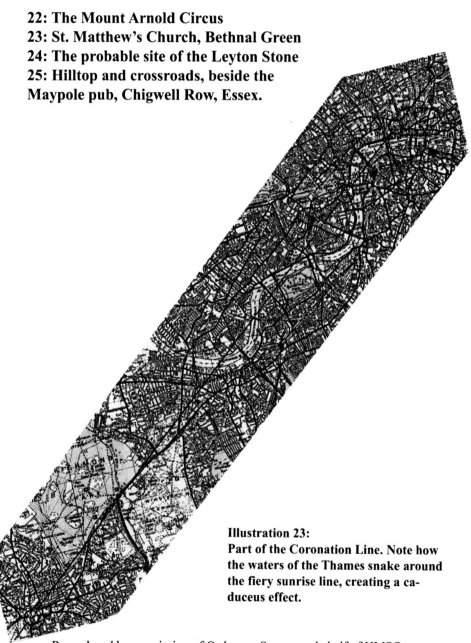

Illustration 23:
Part of the Coronation Line. Note how the waters of the Thames snake around the fiery sunrise line, creating a caduceus effect.

This was an obvious alignment to look for since it includes a straightforward connection between the city's two most well-known sacred sites, Westminster Abbey and St. Paul's Cathedral.

Both have very ancient foundations as places of worship and, according to E.O. Gordon in her 1914 book **Prehistoric London**, both are possible locations of London's lost stone circles.

Take a ride on the London Eye and you can get a spectacular view along the alignment in either direction, using St. Paul's dome or the Abbey as sighting points.

Walking the ley from Shoreditch to Westminster gives a more down-to-earth feel for the alignment and turns up a number of other noteworthy mark points that add weight to the evidence for it; the intriguing mound, disguised as a traffic island at Arnold Circus and the atmospheric ruins of St. Mary Aldermary in Love Lane being two of the most interesting.

On the strength of Westminster Abbey and St. Paul's alone, this looks as if it should be a particularly significant and powerful ley. However, what singles it out as something quite remarkable is the fact that three of its main mark sites are places associated with the coronation of Britain's monarchs. Another four sites are the possible locations of megalithic stones, one of them probably the stone from which Arthur may have drawn his sword of kingship.

Westminster Abbey is, of course, the coronation site we all recognize immediately. For the past 700 years, Britain's monarchs have been crowned here, seated upon the splendid Coronation Throne of Edward Ist. Yet it is not the throne itself which is important but the ancient chunk of stone Edward had built into it, The Stone of Scone.

It might look like an ordinary lump of rock, but it is not.

The Stone of Scone is also known as the Stone of Destiny or Lia

Fail. Prior to it being brought to England by Edward I, it had been the Coronation Stone of the Scottish Kings and before that, the Irish Kings of Tara had been crowned upon it for a thousand years. Its legendary heritage also claims it as a biblical relic, Jacob's prophetic dream stone mentioned in Genesis 28.18. For reasons best known to themselves, John Major's government decided that the stone should be returned to Scotland, so it is no longer at Westminster,

Unique though it may be, it was not the only Coronation Stone on the alignment. To the south west, the line leads like the proverbial arrow, straight to the heart of Kingston-upon-Thames, or more precisely, to All Saints' Church, where, in days gone by, an ancient megalithic monument was housed for many years: The King Stone, from which the town may take its name.

The stone still exists and now stands protected within a small, heptagonal enclosure near the local law courts. Its name derives from the fact that no less than seven Saxon Kings were crowned whilst seated upon it, so Kingston pre-dates Westminster as a coronation site by several hundred years.

The third location, surprisingly, is St. Paul's. It is, of course, a "Royal" church in the sense that it is occasionally chosen for Royal ceremonies, the most important of which in the last century, was the marriage of the Prince and Princess of Wales. However, very few people are aware that St. Paul's is also historically associated with the ancient rituals attached to the coronation of England's Kings.

The land immediately adjacent to the cathedral, was once the place of a folk moot, a form of open air public parliament of national importance, in essence, similar to the one which existed at Parliament Hill, marked by the stone of free speech.

Indeed a similar stone may have existed here in the churchyard of St. Paul's. The folk moot here was eventually marked by a monument known at various times as Old Pol's Cross or Old Pol's Stump. Many old crosses were used to Christianise the site of ancient pagan stones.

Often, the stone was used as the base of the cross and it sounds as if Old Pol's Stump had met this fate, way back in the mists of time.

The coronation connection here is that, amongst the business traditionally discussed openly and resolved at the St. Paul's folk moot, was the election of successive monarchs.

For a great many years, this public election was a vitally important part of the inauguration process and absolutely necessary before any King or Queen could be crowned at Westminster, or anywhere else for that matter.

Edward IV, Stephen, Edward The Confessor, Edmund Ironside and several others are on record as having submitted to this public election prior to their official ceremony and the last monarch to be elected in this way, by open acclamation of the citizens, was Henry III.

So St. Paul's is as important a landmark in the history of the coronation of British Kings, as Westminster Abbey or Kingston's King Stone.

Is it likely to be a coincidence that the three most important mark points on this alignment are all linked to the sovereignty of the land and, more specifically, to the coronation ceremonies of its rulers?

Personally, I don't think so.

The nature and antiquity of the sites suggest this alignment was probably recognised, known and used as far back as the megalithic era.

Another significant clue lies in the orientation of the line.

It appears to be a midsummer sunrise axis.

The solstice sunrise and sunset connection

In simple terms, this orientation means that from Kingston at the dawn of the longest day, the sun would rise in the direction of London, though it is probably not a clear sighting line with the southern heights of Richmond Park in the way.

Similarly, from a point in Westminster, the sun would appear to rise from the vicinity of Ludgate Hill close to where St. Paul's now stands.

Conversely, the view in the opposite direction would mark the alignment of the setting sun at the midwinter solstice, the shortest day.

From Ludgate Hill on the midwinter solstice, the evening sun would sink beyond the horizon in line with Westminster and distant Kingston.

These events would have been of the utmost significance to our ancestors. The frequency with which the midsummer and midwinter solstice alignments are incorporated into the structure of our most ancient monuments, or alignments between them, confirms that.

They may even have been what identified Westminster and Ludgate Hill as London's foremost sacred sites in the first place.

More important, to confirm their relevance to St. Paul's, the midsummer and midwinter solstices are embedded in the history of the the Folk Moot.

Records state it was traditionally held at three times each year; Midsummer (the midsummer solstice) and Christmas (midwinter solstice), were the two most important. The third date, as far as I can remember, is not recorded. I suspect it would have been Beltaine, May 1st.

Here comes The Sun King

A solstice alignment could be the explanation why this line has such strong links to England's Kings and their accession to the throne.

There are known esoteric associations between the sun, as ruler of the heavens, and the monarch as ruler of the land. In many past cultures, the King and the Sun are inextricably intertwined.

The Egyptian Pharaohs, as well as the Inca rulers of South America, were known as Sons of the Sun. To all intents and purposes, they were regarded as the living incarnation of the sun god. Moreover, they took on the mantle of a living sun god at the moment they became ruler, at their coronation or whatever their enthronement ritual was.

In Europe, too, the concept of the divine king existed, most notably in France's Sun King, the flamboyant Louis XIV. It is a universal concept and also embodied in much of the monarch's regalia.

The crown is clearly a solar symbol. It is always gold, the metal associated with the Sun in alchemy, astrology and every other tradition - and the crown's most recognisable features are its radiating spikes, clearly designed to represent the Sun's rays.

The word Coronation even derives from the sun. The corona is the sun's radiance. Coronation literally means crowning with the radiance of the sun.

Clearly, the Coronation line doesn't just create an alignment of sites. It is an axis of power that also somehow esoterically aligns the king with the sun to empower his rule over the land.

Curiously, rulers of all types, whether truly regal or lengths of plastic, share a common etymological root which has given us such words as regal, rex, regina, regulations, la regle (French for ruler), rig (Celtic for King), regime, royal and reich, to name but a few.

Measures in lines and the rule of the sovereign are clearly inter-related concepts from a perspective that might elude most of us today.

Surprisingly, this isn't mere wordplay. It is evident in the ancient Chinese art of Feng Shui, a form of geomancy, 3,000 years old. Feng Shui's natural lines of terrestrial force are not straight. They are serpentine dragon lines, Lung Mei.

However, it does have man-made straight alignments. They only radiate out from the Emperor's palace and are exclusively associated with the ruler of the domain, the human sun at the centre of his universe.

Nearer to home, many of the great palaces and stately homes of Europe's aristocracy appear to have incorporated these esoteric principles into the design and layout of their grounds, so a form of western Feng Shui must have been known and understood - and like China's original, it principally served the chosen few, the ruling elite.

The tradition, whether re-discovered or maintained from earlier times, was taken very seriously by our past ruling classes.

A perfect example is Louis XIV's palace at Versaille. The King's architect, La Notre (also employed by Charles II), laid out the grounds as a solar centre for the French Sun King in the 17th Century.

There is even an example actually on the Coronation Line. Henry VIII's Hampton Court has a long broad avenue directly aligned towards All Saint's Church, the original King Stone site, perhaps to provide his palace with a connection to the stone's (or the line's) sovereign power.

In his classic book, **The Earth Spirit, its Ways, Shrines and Mysteries**, John Michell, the foremost authority on these esoteric subjects, informs us that these landscaping projects were designed following strict geomantic traditions to represent the landowner's power over his domain, whether relating to the King or a member of the local aristocracy.

The Coronation Line is clearly not a simple ley alignment created by man. It represents a power in the land relating directly to the sovereignty of Britain and its people. Its connection to the coronation sites of British monarchs and places associated with the ruling powers of the land make it an extremely important axis of power relative to the entire country, not just the capital.

It is also a royal line, a line of solar power and of the Sun King, or Grail King who rules by divine right (we'll come to King Arthur's role in all this shortly).

Can people or places along this line really exert power and influence over the land and its people ? Surprisingly, the answer is yes. Well .... at Westminster, they can.

The ley can be dowsed at many places along its length, but probably the most appropriate place would be in St. Paul's churchyard near the original site of Old Pol's Cross, described in the St. Paul's Ley Chapter. It has been measured at up to 60 ft wide. Understandably, it would be interesting to see if there are any dowseable changes in the energy, in terms of intensity or line width, at the solstices.

Whilst dowsers might detect a path of solar energy, I do not think that our ancestors would have perceived the power in this alignment as energy. Energy is a relatively modern concept. I believe, they are more likely to have experienced it, as shamans, seers and aboriginal tribe members might, as spirit.

If these alignments serve as spirit paths, it is not necessarily a reference to the spirits of the dead. The principal power in the line is the light of the Sun, so perhaps as a spirit path it carries the soul of the living sun who may be sensed as an apparition of the Sun God (Apollo, Phol, Bel, Lugh ...) or Goddess (Sulis, Minerva, Bride ...).

Surprisingly, in John Michell's book, **Megalithomania**, I found an astonishing reference to just such an occurance at the megalithic site of Callanish on the Isle of Lewis;

" the old people still held certain families in special respect and esteemed as "belonging to the stones" ....The old man also assured him that when the sun rose on Midsummer morning "something" came into the stones, walking down the great avenue, heralded by the cuckoo's call. He had described the "something" by a word (which) was probably pre-Gaelic, and from a root common to the British group of languages. It meant, they thought, the Shining, or Pure, or White one and had probably been the epithet of a god."

Humanity has lost the power to see these visions and the energy currents that cause them, but I believe it is returning.

What would you see coming down this axis of power on midsummer's morning ? Start with what you see on the map.

Look how the course of the Thames weaves around the solar alignment all along its length, alchemically winding the polarities of fire and water into the appearance of a natural, etheric caduceus, or Hermes' rod of power, on the landscape.

It's a potent image. On the inner levels it will be a functional caduceus, too. Maybe, only the divine Grail King could wield that power.

The alignment crosses the Thames seven times from Blackfriar's down to Hampton Court. The number seven suggests a chakra system. That would make Kington the base chakra...and appropriately, St. Paul's, the crown.

Peter Dawkins of the Gatekeeper Trust has been working with a similar Chakra system for a great many years.

St. Paul's King Stone

As I said in a previous chapter, St. Paul is never referred to as Old Pol anywhere else, so I believe the name of Old Pol's Stump or Cross is actually a reference to an older pagan sun god, perhaps Apollo (the druids were known to converse in Greek), or his Saxon counterpart, Phol, more commonly known as Balder in Norse myth.

As a sun stone or King Stone, Old Pol's Stump makes enormous sense. There are well-documented precedents for megalithic King Stones standing on a midsummer sunrise alignment some distance from a main stone circle.

The Hele (helios?) stone at Stonehenge is one. The King Stone at The Rollright Stones megalithic circle in Warwickshire is another. This suggests that E.O. Gordon may have been quite right in her assertion that there could have been a stone circle on Ludgate Hill.

On these assumptions, it would have been located somewhere along the midsummer siting line to the SE of Old Pol's King Stone. That would place it more beneath the tower of the old cathedral than the dome of the present one.

As the King Stone, Old Pol's Stump may have been the sole surviving megalith from this monument. There is a growing conviction, in me at least, that this it may also have been the legendary Arthur's King Stone.

Sir Thomas Mallory in **La Morte D'Arthur** states quite clearly that King Arthur won the divine right to rule by drawing his sword of sovereignty from a stone in the churchyard of *"the greatest church in London."*

In those days, that church would be unquestionably St. Paul's. So the stone must have been the King Stone that became known as Old Pol's Stump, and later Christianised with a cross.

The sword of power Arthur drew from the stone could have been the energy and solar King's power in this alignment, something our megalithic ancestors clearly understood a lot better than we do.

Mallory could only explain it as Merlin's magic and my grasp of it isn't a whole lot better, though I do understand from my Druid background that the term Pendragon is a title, not a name. It means the Head of the Dragon.

So on becoming King, Arthur Pendragon would also became Head of the Dragon Powers of the Land, the dragon being the symbol of the serpentine energy paths which flow through the Earth.

The fact that we have forgotten much of this knowledge is why we are today governed by self-serving fools rather than a wise and knowledgeable Grail King or Queen, able to place the land under a beneficial enchantment.

To sum up; The Coronation Line is an axis of power through both the spiritual and temporal power centres of our Capital.

It is without doubt, the most important ley alignment through the city.

It is a Pendragon Line, a line of power related to the sovereignty of our islands. Its re-discovery is a positive sign that the network built by our megalithic ancestors is re-awakening and re-energising as part of a natural cycle.

I personally believe that the positive energy carried by this ley will wreak beneficial change and havoc on our government and how it operates, however I am willing to admit this may simply be wishful thinking. Time will tell.

Illustrations 24 and 25:
The Rollright Stones in Warwickshire and the King Stone, standing some distance from the stone circle and marking the midsummer sunrise line.

Principal Mark Points

St. George's Hill Weybridge

St. George's Hill is widely known as an exclusive housing estate for the filthy rich and famous. Many household names from the entertainment world live there, amongst the anonymous wealthy.

It qualifies as a valid ley mark point on the evidence that it was once a neolithic hill fort. The association with our dragon-slaying saint, George, is interesting bearing in mind the dragon elements of the last section.

It suggests a place of power where the dragon current was harnessed.

Whiteley's Village Weybridge

This is a curious ley mark point. It's a village specifically created for the elderly at the bequest of William Whiteley, the owner of the once-famous department store in Bayswater.

It was designed as a huge octagon by its consulting architect Walter Cave and interestingly, its SW - NE axis aligns perfectly with the midsummer sunrise orientation of the Coronation Line. The line seems to go through the church on the south side of the village.

Illustration 26:
Whiteley's village is built as an octagon aligned to the Coronation Line.

Wayneflete's Tower Esher

Wayneflete's Tower is a fortified, red-brick four-storey building with semi-octagonal turrets. It was originally the gatehouse to an 11th century Bishop's Palace, The Palace of Esher, on the banks of the River Mole, built by Bishop William Wayneflete.

Sadly in the 17th century, the main manorial buildings, including the keep and the great hall were all demolished and now only the imposing gatehouse remains.

It is strictly private, with no public access.

Grounds of Hampton Court

The alignment cuts across the grounds of Henry VIII's great Palace without interacting with any features of any significance, as far as I can tell from the O.S. map. It passes to the SE of the Stud House and crosses the Long Water close to its central point.

The King Stone and Parish Church of Kingston upon Thames

Presumably, this was an important ritual site in antiquity, otherwise why would there be a large stone here and why would seven successive Saxon Kings have wanted to be crowned whilst sitting upon it.

No clue or remembrance of either the sacred enclosure, monument or traditions survives.

The Kings were Alfred The Great's son, Edward the Elder in 900, followed by Athelstan in 925, Edmund in 940, Eldred (946), Edwy (956), Edward the Martyr (975) and lasty Ethelred II the Unready (979).

The original site of the King Stone is unknown. For many years it stood within the Parish Church, though there have been three of those; the first, All Hallows, the second St. Mary's and the current one, ioutside the Guild Hall in a heptagonal enclosure commemorating the seven Kings.

On a 1;50,000 O.S. map it is debatable whether the alignment passes through the earlier site of the stone (the Parish Church), its present site, or the site of the previous St. Mary's Church somewhere between the two.

Dowsing indicates the site of the Parish church with an outrider of the line to the stone itself.

The King Stone is also one of the most important defining points of the Earthstars 30-point star.

Illustration 27: The current location of The King Stone.

St. Stephen's Church Rochester Row

I've never actually been inside this one. Never passed by when it was open, so can't judge. Looks like a Victorian construction and not on an ancient foundation.

Possible site of the Tothill mound ?

The alignment crosses Horseferry Road in the area which used to be known as Tothill Fields and quite close to the location where David Furlong and other researchers suggest the Tothill Mound may-have stood (see earlier chapter on Watkins' fourth Ley).

St. Matthew's Church Great Peter Street

A traditional Victorian Gothic stone church, just around the corner from Westminster Abbey and almost lost between modern developments.

I've never been inside this one either, but I am told the interior is well worth a visit.

Westminster Abbey

This alignment passes through the abbey between Edward the Confessor's shrine and the crossing point of nave and transept, quite noticably the most vibrant part of the buildng energetically. I wonder whether the temple of Apollo was here and whether this solar alignment empowered it. For more information on Westminster Abbey, see the Stonehenge Line chapter.

St. Margaret's Westminster

I had always wondered why St. Margaret's had been sited so close to Westminster Abbey. The official reason is that it was built by the Benedictine Monks in the 12th century, so that local people who lived in the area around the Abbey could worship separately at their own simpler parish church; a more considerate alternative to putting a 'No riff-raff' sign up at the Abbey entrance.

There may be another, more esoteric explanation, of course. There are no records of what may have occupied Margaret's site initially, but what if it was another King Stone, outlying the stone circle that is supposed to have been on the site of the abbey ?

It would have stood directly on the midsummer sunrise alignment, a short distance to the NE of the abbey, like St. Margaret's. Was the most important stone in the megalithic temple once positioned somewhere near where St. Margaret's now stands?

And why St. Margaret ? My explanation is that St. Margaret is the female equivalent of St. George. She is a dragon-slaying saint. It would make perfect sense to Christianise the principal mark point of this powerful pendragon alignment with one of the church's dragon slayers.

Incidentally, slaying the dragon is a symbolic, geomantic act that pins the energy at one spot to enable it to be re-directed or otherwise utilised.The Normans were experts at this kind of thing.

Their crusade of construction which resulted in so many of our cathedrals, abbeys, churches and castles, clearly demonstrates they were putting into practice a complex system of geomantic knowledge, though it was clearly hidden knowledge as far as the common man was concerned and generally still is, to this day.

It's time for it to be out in the open and acknowledged.

Blackfriar's Monastery

The alignment goes directly through Blackfriar's Station and the site of the Blackfriar's Monastery.

From 1221 to 1538 the Blackfriars Monastery was located on the riverside. It was a wealthy and influential institution, and like many other sites along this axis of power, it was frequently used for government council meetings. The so-called "Black Parliament" met there prior to the start of the Wars of the Roses. After the dissolution of the monasteries in the 16th century, the site was home to the Blackfriars Playhouse and the area eventually became a fashionable residential district.

St. Andrew's-by-the-Wardrobe and St. Ann's Blackfriars

The wardrobe is not an Ikea item dumped in the churchyard. It was Edward III's clothes store which occupied an entire building nearby.

The church's history pre-dates it considerably (earliest mention 1170) and probably commenced with a chapel of the Blackfriars' monastery dedicated to St. Ann. It is interesting how St. Ann may have been an early gender re-alignment case to become St. Andrew, possibly at a time when female saints were not in favour.

St. Andrew's in Totteridge was also originally dedicated to a female saint, Etheldreda.

St. Andrews-by-the-Wardrobe is by Wren and feels rather bare, empty and lacking in soul. The accoustics are good though, so on my last visit, I sang it up a bit.

The alignment passes through the altar end of the building.

St. Paul's Cathedral

The summit of Ludgate Hill, where St. Paul's now stands is probably the earliest and most important sacred site in the capital. It is a place steeped in tradition, rich in history and legend, a place of free speech and public parliament, such as was practiced at Parliament Hill. A place where laws were decreed, justice dispensed and kings elected. Its associations with the mythic foundation of London and its temple of Diana makes it a place of legend and vision.

The present cathedral, built by Sir Christopher Wren, is at least the third to occupy the site, possibly the fourth. All of the previous buildings were destroyed by fire.

The first church recorded here dates back to 604AD and was built for the first Bishop of the East Saxons, Mellitus, who came from Rome with Augustine, on a mission to convert Engand's pagan Saxons to Christianity, totally ignoring the fact that the Apostolic church of Glastonbury had been Christian for the previous five hundred years.

A famous letter from Augustine to Mellitus instructs him not to destroy pagan temples but to **"re-consecrate them to the true god"**. The Cathedral's associations with a temple of Diana suggest it was the site of one such temple.

When Wren re-built the cathedral following the Great Fire of 1666, it was the key location in his plan to re-create the city as the spiritual center of the world, the New Jerusalem. Its precise height, 365 feet, mirrors the number of days in our annual orbit of the sun and its other dimensions and proportions embody much cosmological symbolism and significance, now obscured by the meaningless metric system.

It is, without a shadow of a doubt, the most important sacred site in the city and the focus of more one ley alignment, though I suspect the Coronation Line is the most powerful.

Does the alignment's associations with the sun god, Apollo (Old Pol), or the Saxon's Phol, sit uncomfortably with the notion of a temple dedicated to the lunar goddess, Diana? It depends which came first. The obvious contender would be a megalithic monument and its alignments. As Professor Lockyer, Professor Thom, John Michell, Robin Heath and others have shown, these normally incorporate both solar and lunar observation lines.

As for later temples, sacred hills often share their summits with many different gods and Ludgate Hill is no exception. An old (1828) book in my possession entitled **Londiniana** by Edward Wedlake Brayley, adds Jupiter to the list of deities whose temples formerly graced the locality of St. Paul's.

"Bishop Stillingfleet, who in his "Discourses on the true Antiquity of London and its state in Roman times" - published in the 2d part of his "Ecclesiastical Cases" - considered a temple of Jupiter rather than Diana, to have stood on the eminence which St. Paul's now occupies."

In the same chapter, Brayley comments:

"Tradition has long rendered the opinion that the Romans had a Temple for pagan worship on the site of the present Cathedral of St. Paul; yet whether it was dedicated to Jupiter or Diana, or whether such a building existed at all has never been satisfactorily ascertained."

He also raises the suggestion that the name London derives from *Llan Din,* which his source quotes as meaning *'The sacred place of Diana.'* I had never heard this idea before. It is translated as *'The High Sacred Eminence'* by E.O.Gordon in her book, or the less likely *'settlement by the lake'* by others.

On the question of Diana, Jupiter or Apollo, I personally sense the presence of both male and female deities in the area. For more on St. Paul's, see the St. Paul's Ley chapter.

The site of Old Pol's Stump

As previously mentioned, this is the possible site of a megalithic King Stone set up to mark the midsummer sunrise siting line through a stone circle on Ludgate Hill.

It could also be Arthur's legendary King Stone from which he drew the sword of sovereignty. See also the St. Paul's Ley chapter as the two alignments intersect at this point.

St. Vedast-alias-Foster, Foster Lane

Walk from Old Pol's Cross to the NE gate of St. Paul's churchyard. Just across the road, sandwiched between two modern office blocks, you will see St. Vedast's which has been a place of worship since the 12th Century.

Don't miss the small peaceful courtyard on the north side of the church, a great place to meditate or simply soak up the atmosphere.

As we're following a line associated with Coronation, Royalty and so on, it may be no coincidence that set into the south wall of the courtyard is a stone dedicated to "The King of the World".

St. Mary Aldermanbury, Love Lane

This is a beautiful spot, a tiny oasis of greenery in the concrete desert of the city. It stands on an ancient sacred foundation first mentioned in 1181, so was probably built upon an earlier pre-Christian site.

Only the bases of the walls and columns still stand. The church was first destroyed by the Great Fire in 1666, then Wren's rebuilt model was flattened by the Blitz in 1940, leaving only the walls.

In 1966 its shattered remains were shipped to Fulton, Missouri, by the residents of that town, and rebuilt in the grounds of Westminster College, Missouri, as a memorial to Sir Winston Churchill. Churchill had made his Sinews of Peace, "Iron Curtain" speech from the College in 1946.

A strong Marian presence may be felt in these gardens near where the church's altar would have been. Also it is thought that the Victorian drinking fountain on the corner and in line with the altar may mark the site of a holy spring or well previsouly associated with the site. Whether this is correct or not is yet to be confirmed.

Illustration 28:
The splendid oasis formed by the remains of St. Mary Aldermanbury, at the corner of Love Lane.

The Mount Arnold Circus

If you've read the earlier chapter on Watkins' Strand Ley, you know everything there is to know about the mysterious mount.

The Coronation line passes to the east of the mound, rather than directly through it. The mound may have extended that far before it was levelled. Leys are known to connect with circular monuments at a tangent to their circumference, as well as through their centres, or anywhere else for that matter, so it doesn't make that much difference.

The site of the Leyton Stone ?

This could be yet another old stone on this alignment. The Leyton Stone managed to avoid being turned into the base for a cross, though in the 18th Century an obelisk was mounted on top of it. You'll find it near the junction of Hollybush Hill and New Wanstead. It has been suggested that it is the remains of a Roman milestone, but it could be older. As usual there's no solid evidence one way or another.

It's worth mentioning High Road Leytonstone is claimed to be a prehistoric pathway dating from before the Roman period, so where it coincides with this alignment may be significant as Alfred Watkins would have counted an aligned section of old track or pathway as a mark point in itself.

A little back further down the alignment is another significant site for a midsummer sunrise line. Leytonstone's St. John's Parish Church which stands on a very ancient foundation, not directly on theline, but close to it.

The church's dedication is entirely appropriate for this midsummer sunrise alignment since St. John's day is June 24th, within the period of the midsummer solstice when the sun rises at its highest northern point on the horizon for 3 consecutive days.

The Maypole Pub and crossroads, Chigwell Row, Essex

The name of the local pub here suggests the existence of an old ritual site where gatherings took place on at least one day of the year, May Day or Beltaine.

Evidence from the alignments seems to support this hypothesis.

A Mayday sunrise line through here would align back to a very significant point, one of London's sacred hills, Primrose Hill. Equally significant is the fact that the Mayday alignment runs directly along the course of the approach road to the junction from the West.

Ancient crossroads were considered powerful places for pre-Christian ritual activity and this one seems to be located at an important junction of two alignments, both related to major pagan festivals, a Mayday sunrise line and a Midsummer sunrise line.

If Mayday, one of the eight Celtic 'wheel of the year' festivals, was celebrated here, it is probable that other rituals were, too.

That a midsummer sunrise alignment crosses here, as well, from a significant number of London's other sacred sites, could mark it as an important forgotten ceremonial location.

The Maypole itself is at the crown of the hill, but a modern sacred site, All Saint's Church, is less than 50 yards down the road.

It dates only from the Victorian era but has an interesting atmosphere and a churchyard full of yews, the Celtic tree of life, rebirth and renewal.

Chapter Ten

The Sacred Hills of London

Parliament Hill Ley

Mark sites

1: Summit of Parliament Hill 2: Summit of Highgate Hill 3: Site of The High Gate 4: St. Joseph's Chapel Highgate School 5: Alexandra Palace Hill 6: Remains of Bronze Age camp at the summit of Bush Hill Enfield 7: Site of Eliza bethan Palace at Enfield 8: St. Andrew's Parish Church Enfield.

Here we have an alignment which includes five of North London's most prominent hills, at least three of them with ancient history.

If we begin the line at Parliament Hill, it rises to the exact summit of Highgate Hill, passes through what would have been the Hermit's Gate at the top of the hill beside the Gatehouse Pub, then crosses the road, to enter Highgate School through its chapel, now dedicated to St. Joseph, but originally Highgate's first parish church dedicated then to St. Michael.

Dropping over the hill behind, it goes through Queen's Wood and on up to Alexandra Palace, perched atop another of London's hills. Here the alignment runs the length of the palace then continues to the top of Bush Hill Enfield, site of a half-destroyed Bronze-Age camp of the Cattuvellaunii tribe, now on a golf course.

The final points are Enfield's old St. Andrew's in the Market Square and the site of an Elizabethan Palace of which nothing remains but the memory in the name of 'the Palace Gardens' Shopping Centre.

115

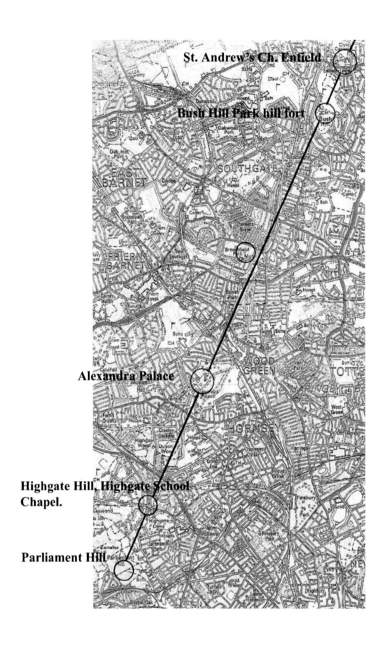

Illustration 29: The Sacred Hills of London - Parliament Hill Ley.

Reproduced by permission of Ordnance Survey on behalf of HMSO.
Crown Copyright. All rights reserved. Licence number; 10029558.

Parliament Hill

The late Ross Nichols, former Chosen Chief of the Order of Bards Ovates and Druids tells us in **The Book of Druidry** that Parliament Hill was once marked by the ditches and ramparts of a Bronze-Age camp. The earthworks have long since disappeared, but were said to have still been in evidence as recently as the early Victorian era.

Descriptions of them must have existed somewhere, because Ross was able to form the opinion that their design would have been ineffectual as defensive measures and that they must have served instead to create a sacred enclosure.

E.O. Gordon's **Prehistoric London** supports this with the information that the old name for Parliament Hill was the Llan Din, which means "sacred high eminence." Perhaps the 'high place of the gods' relative to the whole area.

The place still has definite druid associations, with the Stone of Free Speech marking the site of a traditional open-air druid parliament (which gives the hill its modern name) on the east side of the hill.

Tradition has it that Boudicca used the camp with her army before swooping down towards London to engage the Romans at Battle Bridge (a bridge over the River Fleet in the vicinity of King's Cross). Supposedly, her remains are buried beneath platform 9 at King's Cross.

Another version of the tale, favoured by Sir Montague Sharpe, is that her last battle with Gaius Seutonius Paulinus took place on the northern edge of the heath and that Boudicca's tumulus to the north of Parliament Hill is her final resting place.

There are many magical spots on Hampstead Heath and the top of Parliament Hill isn't necessarily the best of them. Yet, looking out over the view down to the city and the Thames, you can still get a sense of this as a high place of power in the past and as a much-needed natural sanctuary in the suburbs today.

Illustration 30 (top): Boudicca's Mound on Hampstead Heath.

Illustration 31: St. Joseph's Chapel, Highgate School. Site of the original Parish Church of Highgate.

118

Highgate Hill

Ross Nichols was convinced that the summit of Highgate Hill was previously the site of a druidic college, vaguely recalled in the several street names still called groves.

The tradition of higher education continues with Highgate School perched atop London's highest hill.

The Druid college connection is taken a stage further by John Michell, a leading authority on such matters, who maintained that the locations of many of our prominent public schools, including Eton (which he attended himself), Harrow, Mill Hill School, Marlborough School and so on, occupy the previous sites of former druidic centres of learning.

The alignment at Highgate passes directly over the summit of the hill, through the school and through its school chapel, dedicated to St. Joseph.

This had been the first Parish Church of Highgate and originally dedicated to St. Michael, prior to the construction of the Victorian St. Michael's in South Grove.

Alfred Watkins would have been delighted to find that this alignment approaches St. Joseph's via another verifiable ley mark point. It follows a straight section of Highgate West Hill past the Flask Pub, thus confirming its potential as part of the old straight track.

More important, it would also have originally passed through "The High Gate" kept traditionally by a local hermit (Hermes – guardian of the ways, remember ?)

Nowadays the Hermitage has been replaced by The Gate House pub.

Alexandra Palace Hill

Some people believe that Alexandra Palace's tendency to catch fire repeatedly was due to its location on a troublesome ley line and a fiery pagan temple to the sun which it is supposed to have been built upon.

According to local newspapers, when the place was undergoing its last redevelopment, the management brought in the well-known astrologer and psychic Russell Grant, to try to fix the problem. I am not sure what he did, but according to the report, it involved burying some copper rods and crystals in an attempt to cure the problem.

Ally Pally is actually on a number of leys, but they are not necessarily the cause of the problem. When the original Palace was built, a local wise-woman, only known as Old Rose, was evicted from her tumble-down home at the top of the hill. As a result, she placed a curse on the development and before the building was a month old, it burnt to the ground.

Interestingly, some of the roads and boundaries around the palace form a very hag-like profile.

Local psychics report that the spirit of the witch has returned to make sure that the proposed new development does not destroy the atmosphere of the hill which was seemingly a sacred place in the distant past, where the eternal flame of Bride or Bridget burnt on the summit and with shrines and springs dedicated to Diana/Artemis on its eastern slopes.

Interestingly, the current building exhibits many features more appropriate to the sacred architecture of a temple, including the huge rose window - which utilises the geometry of the London Earthstars' mandala - and a winged female statue of an angel or a goddess figure, standing guardian from the rooftop.

If I were one of the trustees of the development, I would take care not to offend the spirit of the witch in case she decides their efforts should go up in smoke again.

The alignment here runs the length of the building, from the main front entrance to the small rear car park, directly along the same axis as the palace, but off-centre to the South East side.

Alexandra Palace features on this ley and the Whetstone Ley later in the book. It is also on a line of The Earthstars five-point star, running from St. Mary's in East Barnet to Bellingham Green in SE London, via Highbury Hill and Tower Hill.

Illustration 32:
Alexandra Palace, where the rose window is based on the same geometry as Stonehenge and the London Earthstars matrix.

Some old straight track

Curiously the alignment runs directly along a lengthy section of perfectly straight rail track between Alexandra Palace and Winchmore Hill. I have no idea whether this was an old straight track of a different sort before the railway was built. It could be simply a coincidence.

Bush Hill Park bronze age encampment

The alignment crosses the fairways and greens of Bush Hill Park Golf Cub. From whichever direction you come, it's up a steep incline and in the distant past, you would have been climbing the ramparts of a sizeable hill fort, not trudging up a road in a middle-class suburb.

Not many people know that this was the site of a Bronze Age encampment of the Belgic Cattuvellauni tribe who inhabited these parts (and much of Hertfordshire and Middlesex) prior to the Roman period.

There are no obvious signs of the usual deep ditches or lofty earthworks. The only visible evidence is behind the clubhouse where some of the banks still remain. However, according to Sir Montague Sharpe in his book on the antiquities of Middlesex, in the early 1900s the near circular earthworks were 150 ft in diameter and three quarters of them were still intact. As he also states that they enclosed the house and its lawns (which now serves as the club house) presumably they were levelled when the golf course was created. There could be a few bronze age bunkers out there.

The earliest records of Winchmore Hill call it Wynsemerhull, which translates as boundary hill. This encampment and the prominent hilltop it stood upon could have been the boundary hill that gave the area it's name. There was a simlar encampment in Hadley Wood, to the east of the railway bridge on the footpath from the bottom of Baker's Lane. Here the footpath follows the bottom of one of the steep embankments of the camp, but sadly, very little else of it remains.

Enfield Palace

In Elizabethan times, a palace stood on the south side of what is now Enfield High Street. Very little is known about it and nothing remains. It is only remembered in the name of the modern shopping precinct; the Palace Gardens' Shopping Centre.

St. Andrew's, the Parish Church of Enfield

This is a lovely old church and a lovely old churchyard whose wildlife, greenery and air of country quiet contrasts pleasantly with the rest of Enfield town centre, which is noisy, dirty, and often very crowded.

The alignment crosses the High Street and the Market Square to enter the church, which is a very ancient place of worship.

The first written evidence of a Parish Church here dates from 1136, when St Andrew's, along with a number of other neighbouring parishes was endowed to Walden Abbey in Essex, now Audley End House, Saffron Walden.

It's believed there was an earlier church on the site way back in the Saxon era, but there are no records of it.

This is the only point on the alignment that isn't a lofty hill.

Chapter Eleven

The Sacred Hills of London

Primrose Hill Ley

Mark sites

**1: Summit of Primrose Hill 2: St. Michael's Highgate Hill
3: Summit of Highgate Hill   4: St. Joseph's Chapel High
gate School 5: Summit of Muswell Hill 6: Muswell Hill
Methodist Church 7: Christ Church Southgate - site of The
Weld Chapel and Minchenden Oak.**

Even with crowds of people on the summit, Primrose Hill is a
magical place. I always feel it is more of a goddess site than Parliament
Hill and have had several unusual experiences here.

The first was to find that as I walked up the hill, I could sense
each chakra from the base to the crown, energising one by one as I
walked to the crown of the hill. The second was a vision of Primrose
Hill as a hill of light.

It was on an occason when I had watched the winter solstice
sunrise on Parliament Hill, then rushed over to Primrose Hill, to see
what the view looked like from there.

I was in for a shock. Normally, I would park in Primrose Hill
Rd and walk up the hill from the gate near Ainger Rd. This time, for no
particular reason, I ignored the habits of a lifetime, parked on the north
side of the hill near the shops and walked past St. Mary's church and in
through the King Henry's Road gate. What made me do this, I don't
know, but as soon as I looked up at the hill, I realised that my subconscious actions were not without reason.

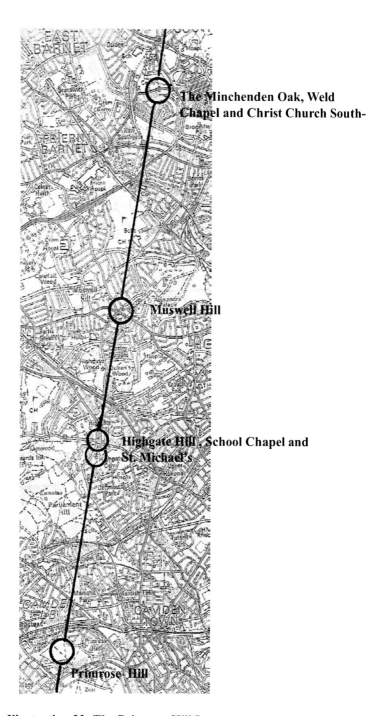

The Minchenden Oak, Weld
Chapel and Christ Church South-

Muswell Hill

Highgate Hill, School Chapel and
St. Michael's

Primrose Hill

Illustration 33: The Primrose Hill Ley

As I walked up the path, the whole hill was ablaze, with the sun sitting right on the summit. For a moment, time stood still and I drifted back to a time when this was a regular place of ritual. I imagined a group of druids atop the hill, then saw how the sun would rise out of the ground or perhaps even roll up the side of the hill to engulf them. Seemingly carrying them off into the sky to return at some later date from the land of the gods and to the amazement of their people.

I felt sure that it had been part of the ancient ceremonies enacted at this site by our ancestors and that St. Mary's church the end of King Henry's Road could mark the place of the gathering where the scenes may be observed.

I walked up the hill, feeling as if I was literally walking into the centre of the blazing sun and being totally re-energised.

At the summit, the illusion disappeared. Yet I felt totally overwhelmed by the experience. I felt myself becoming part of the sun's energy, being engulfed by the light. I entered the sun and the sun entered me, shone through me, illuminating every cell of my being with power and energy.

I had been ill with a minor infection and I felt as if all the illness was being burnt out of my body. As the sun rose higher, I gradually returned to everyday consciousness. But the amazing sense of empowerment remained. I felt renewed, invigorated, totally alive and reborn. The winter solstice is a celebration of the rebirth of the sun and I had shared in the experience.

I sat down for a while and imagined how our ancestors would have reacted to this phenomenon.

From the bottom of the hill, anyone walking up to the summit would literally have walked into the sun and have been engulfed by it. Possibly, they could have created the illusion of being lifted up to the heavens when it rose higher. Taken by the light. I wondered if this illusion had been part of the rituals enacted here in the past.

126

As I stood on the summit, I had felt literally engulfed by the power of the sun. I had become one with the light and felt as if I had been born again from it. In that respect, it would have been no illusion. It was a magical experience, a visitation and communion with the sun, or with the son of the sun, for these forces sometimes take human form for the mystic or the shaman.

This initiation into the mysteries of Primrose Hill is one of the most amazingly invigorating and enlightening experiences I have ever had. I often revisit it in meditation whenever I feel in need of energy.

Anyway, back to the ley. From the top of Primrose Hill, you may be able to see the spire of St. Michael's on Highgate Hill and from this siting line work out where the alignment crosses the hill.

Interesting that the alignment at Highgate takes in the current Parish Church, St. Michael's, as well as the original St. Joseph's, now the school chapel. Makes you wonder whether St. Michael's builders deliberately sited it on the alignment.

Actually, this line might not have been considered a valid ley by Watkins. The churches along it's length are all post-reformation which leaves only three hills as mark points, plus the chapel at Highgate which may have been preceded in very ancient times by a wooden chapel attached to the Hermitage.

Meaningful alignments can obviously be found, marked by fairly recent buildings of the sort you would expect to find on a ley and wth dowsable energy paths.

Does that mean the buildings stand on ancient sites we no longer remember, or that the Victorians who built these places, were aware of the alignments ? I am certain in some cases they were.

Or does it mean that the soul energy of a place or the energy of an alignment, somehow inspires people to locate certain buildings in alignment subconsciously ?

Primrose Hill

Primrose Hill is closely associated with Druids, in modern times, if not the distant past. It is alleged that John Toland began the Druid revival by gathering all British Druids at the Autumn Equinox on Primrose Hill in 1717. By this act, he created the Universal Bond of Druids (An Druidh Uileach Braithreachas) from which the largest Druid Order in modern times, The Order of Bards Ovates and Druids, has evolved.

The Universal Bond of Druids still exists separate to OBOD and still celebrates the Autumn Equinox every year upon the summit of Primrose Hill, with a traditional Druid ceremony. I participated in the ceremony myself several times in the early 90s.

John Toland's foundation myth is a romantic narrative without historical basis, according to Ronald Hutton, Professor of History at Bristol University. Toland though is remembered for three other reasons. 1: He coined the term pantheism. 2: His book entitled **Christianity Not Mysterious** was ordered to be publicly burnt. 3: For his most famous quotation;

"The Sun is my father, the Earth my mother, the world is my country and all men are my family."

Other Druidic associations with the hill are linked to Iolo Morganwg, the legendary Welsh poet and Visionary Bard, who on the summer solstice of 1792 inaugurated the first Bardic Gorsedd - you guessed it - on Primrose Hill. These days, it is more often celebrated in Wales where it has become The Welsh National Eisteddfod.

A plaque (of welsh slate) commemorating this was unveiled at Primrose Hill on the Summer Solstice 2009.

The connection between the Welsh Druids and Britain, in case you are wondering, is that The Welsh are the ancient Britons.

One final thing to look out for at Primrose Hill is in the London A-Z Streetfinder. It shows clearly that the footpaths of the park form a pentagram pointing to the top of the hill.

Local folklore has it that if you walk the pentagram, you will be blessed with a vision, long life and cured of all ailments.

No-one knows where this tale originated and as far as I know, it is not written down anywhere. I was told it, one day, by an old lady who was sitting on one of the benches at the top of the hill. I haven't tried it myself.

St. Michael's Parish Church South Grove Highgate

A Victorian Gothic edifice built in 1832, designed by Lewis Vulliamy. It claims to be the highest church in London though I suspect the next mark point on the line, St. Joseph's Chapel at Highgate School, is a couple of feet higher. St. John's Church at Barnet will certainly be higher, but that may be considered to be outside London.

The alignment here passes across Pond Square, where it meets at least one other ley. Sadly the spring that fed the pond has been capped off and Pond Square is now pondless.

St. Joseph's Chapel on the summit of Highgate Hill

This is a much older site than I first thought. Local history tells us that at the time of William the Conqueror, nearly a thousand years ago, the Bishop of London appointed a priest here and gave him eight acres of land at the very top of the hill, so that a chapel and lodging for the priest could be built there for services.

A simple wooden chapel was built and as time passed, it became the chapel of the village, being replaced by a more substantial building in 1578 which lasted until 1833.

Presumably the current school chapel replaced it as, by then, the new St. Michael's Parish Church had been completely a short distance away in South Grove.

Summit of Muswell Hill

The alignment here passes directly over the summit of the hill at the bus terminus traffic island in Muswell Hill Broadway, just before the road plummets down to Crouch End and Hornsey.

Muswell Hill takes its name from a sacred site, the Mosse Well or Mossy Well, which some claim as a source of the Moselle Brook that flows through Tottenham into Pymmes Brook, and then on to the River Lee.

I had always thought the name could have just as easily derived from the Muse Well, implying the spectral presence of a "White Lady" or "Grail Maiden of the Well" traditionally asociated with healing wells and springs. You never know. Whatever its name, it made the hill a place of pilgrimage in mediaeval times as its waters were indeed reputed to have miraculous healing properties.

Tradition has it that a Scottish King was cured of serious disease after taking the waters of the well. What his symptoms were or even what his name was are ommitted from the tale.

Nevetheless, this is an ancient sacred hill, where nuns in the 12th century built a chapel dedicated to "Our Lady of Muswell, " so perhaps there had been apparitions at the well and it did have a muse or Grail Maiden after all.

No-one is certain where the nun's original chapel would have been, but a well still exists in the front garden of a house named RoseDale in Muswell Avenue. I am told it's the Mosse/Muse Well, but haven't yet found any confirmation of the fact.

Muswell Hill Baptist Church

Most of Muswell Hill was largely undeveloped until the latter part of the nineteenth century, so its churches are no older than a hundred years or so. This one is a late Victorian red brick construction perched on the brow of the Hill in Duke's Rd. There is no mention in any records of anything significant previously on the site, but then, in the distant past, the whole area of the summit may have been an ancient Holy Hill, especially if it had a sacred well.

The interior of the church has a really good atmosphere.

Christ Church Southgate, The Weld Chapel and The Minchenden Oak

The alignment continues directly to the area of Christ Church, near Old Southgate Green.

Ostensibly this is a Victorian Church of no great antiquity as a sacred site. I suspect otherwise. Slightly to the west of the church, in Waterfall Road, is a small walled garden, location of The Weld Chapel, first built in 1615. All that remains of it is a few stones and the bases of several pillars.

More significantly, next to it is something that may be a clue to the real origins of this place as a sacred site.

It is an absolutely massive tree known as The Minchenden Oak, and by the look of it, over a thousand years old.

The local history section of Palmers Green library has references to a notable tree in this area in the late 1500s that was known as "The Seven Sisters" the name originating from the fact that the tree's vast trunk divided into seven offshoots.

This tree also has seven trunks branching off from its main massive base, so it is probably the same tree. Another one wouldn't have grown to this size in just a couple of hundred years, that's for sure.

In 1873, it was said to be the largest in England with a girth of over 27 feet, its canopy spread *'no less than 126 feet, and still growing'*. It is believed to be over 800 years old.

The name suggests it was considered to be a venerated tree, possibly associated with a nearby shrine or having some local spiritual significance.

Nearby, on Southgate Green in the 1500s was the house known as Arnold's Grove from which the name Arnos Grove evolved.

Arnos Grove was, until the dissolution of the monasteries by Henry VIII, owned by the Nuns of Clerkenwell. It was known as Armholt Wood in the 14th century, and later as Arnolds.

The tree stood within grounds of Arnold's Grove House.

Could it have been part of a druid grove that gave the house its name ?

Several other alignments pass through here. At least one of them significantly passes through the area near the tree, not the church or chapel.It is an Earthstars five-point star line to St. Mary's East Barnet.

The garden where The Minchenden Oak stands and the Weld Chapel remains lie, is secluded and tranquil. It's an ideal place to sit in search of inspiration or to see what you pick up psychically about the events of the past here.

And if you are into talking to trees, you may find The Minchenden Oak has an interesting tale or two to tell.

Illustration 34:
The Weld Chapel, Southgate's first place of Christian
worship. Its ruins can be seen in the walled garden beside Christ Church.

Illustration 35:
The Minchenden Oak, a huge and wonderful tree beside the ruins of The Weld
Chapel. Does it mark the site of a forgotten druid grove or shrine ?

Chapter Twelve

The Whetstone Ley

Mark sites

1: **St. John's on the crest of Barnet Hill (also through the Spiritualist Church in Union Street)**
2: **The Whetstone in Whetstone High Street**
3: **A straight section of Friern Barnet Lane**
4: **St. James' Church Friern Barnet**
5: **Church path and gate on the ley**
6: **Friary Park - gate and path on the ley**
7: **Site of the Manor House/Friary in Friary Park**
8: **Statute of Peace in Friary Park**
9: **Alexandra Palace**
10: **Finsbury Park**
11: **St. John The Evangelist Queens Drive N4**
12: **St. James' Stoke Newington High Street**
13: **National Maritime Museum Greenwich**
14: **Greenwich Park - site of Roman Temple**
15: **Chislehurst.**

Here's another line that passes through Alexandra Palace. This is a classic ley that conforms to many features noted by Watkins in **The Old Straight Track**.

It starts on an impressive hilltop marked by a pre-reformation church, includes another very old church and several more recent ones, follows a straight stretch of road and a church path directly through a gate in the churchyard, traces the route of an underground tunnel and another path, to the site of the former local manor and Friary - and includes three other hilltops, a royal palace, a Roman temple and

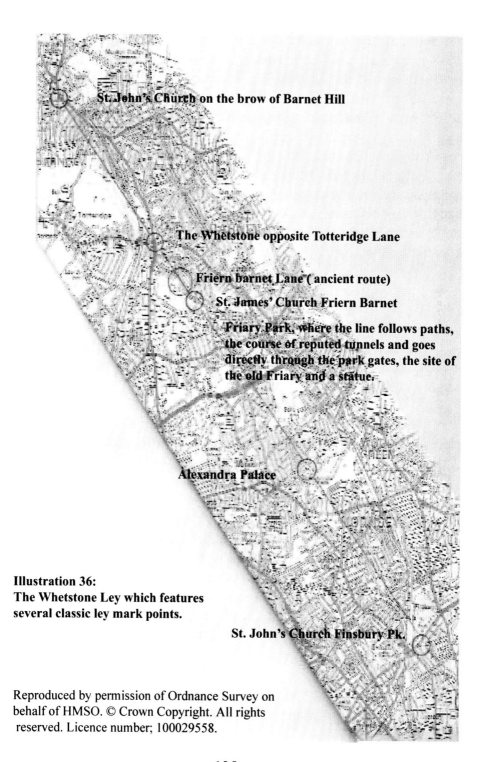

St. John's Church on the brow of Barnet Hill

The Whetstone opposite Totteridge Lane

Friern barnet Lane (ancient route)

St. James' Church Friern Barnet

Friary Park, where the line follows paths, the course of reputed tunnels and goes directly through the park gates, the site of the old Friary and a statue.

Alexandra Palace

Illustration 36:
The Whetstone Ley which features
several classic ley mark points.

St. John's Church Finsbury Pk.

a well of unknown antiquity along its route. It also features one of London's rare old stones, The Whetstone, set into the pavement outside the Griffin Pub on Whetstone High Road opposite Totteridge Lane.

Local historians dispute The Whetstone's origins but its presence on this alignment with sites of notable antiquity raises the distinct possibility that this could be a genuine remnant of a megalithic monument. After all, in parts of the country where more of our megalithic heritage survives, the majority of ley mark points are actually stones like this. But before we examine the various theories about the whetstone, let's trace the alignment's defining points, beginning with the impressive church of St. John which dominates the crest of Barnet Hill.

St. John's Barnet Hill

This is actually, the highest point in the London suburbs. There is even a plaque in the church that tells you the altar is at the same height as the top of the dome of St. Paul's Cathedral.

In the days when the gods were deemed to dwell in the high places, this would have been the most sacred spot for miles around.

Most histories of Barnet tell us the name derives simply from a burnt or cleared space in the forest. I don't think so. There is an Old English word 'beorg' or 'beorh' that could have lent itself to the first part of Barnet's name and means, appropriately a high place, in particular a sacred high place and possibly a burial mound. I think that fits better with Barnet's new role as a high place of the ancient gods. Sir Montague Sharpe's book on Middlesex in ancient times tells us that Chipping Barnet and East Barnet were actually called Sudhaw, meaning south enclosure, though in other parts of the country, the word haw or how is used to describe a mound or barrow.

St. John's Church dates from the 12th Century and was almost certainly a chapel of ease to the Mother Church of the area, the picturesque little hilltop church of St. Mary's in East Barnet. St. John's had been built by Michaelmas 1276 because a court roll entry refers to *"an obstruction on the road leading to the church of Barnet and the market."* Nevertheless, it did not become a separate parish church for another six hundred years.

Illustration 37:
The Parish Church of St. John's which dominates the view from the crest of Barnet Hill.

The Whetstone

There are numerous theories about the origins of The Whetstone. One is that it was a stone used by soldiers to sharpen their swords during the Civil War. That may be true but it doesn't explain how the stone came to be there or what its original purpose was.

Another explanation is that it was used by ladies as they dismounted from coaches or horses at the Griffin when it was a Coaching Inn. Again this may be true but could be merely an opportune use of a conveniently placed stone. A third idea is that it was the "west" stone marking the boundary of the lands owned by the monks of Friern Barnet whose religious house is another mark point further down this line.

The most credible explanation comes from Sir Montague Sharpe who points out that the Whetstone (originally the Whitestone) is a boundary marker sited on a grid system probably laid out by a Roman survey. I prefer the notion that it is an earlier ancient megalithic mark stone, possibly the only one remaining from a large monument at this location. There's no solid evidence for this, of course, except the fact that the stone sits precisely on several other ley alignments, one of them connecting to another old stone in the London suburbs. It also sits on an important line of the Earthstars geometry; a chord of the ten point star from St. Mary's East Barnet to the Burnt Oak point at Watling Park. Remarkably, the same line can be extended in both directions to connect up to points of the 30 point star, so forming another chord of that. Not a coincidence, I am sure. The honest answer to the question of what the Whetstone might have been though, is we don't know for sure. It is all a matter of personal opinion.

What we do know is that in the 14th century, the Bishop of London permitted a new road to be constructed on his land, to the west of Friern Barnet. The new route was called the King's Highway and eventually became known as the Great North Road. Whether the Whetstone had stood in an open field or alongside an earlier existing trackway, prior to this development, we'll never know, but certainly the term

Illustration 38:
The enigmatic Whetstone, set into the pavement opposite
Totteridge Lane, on Whetstone High Rd.

'The King's Highway' pre-dates this route and the stone itself seems quite unique. No other "stepping stones" for ladies or a "sharpening stones" for swordsmen have survived alongside the road.

Friern Barnet Lane

From the Whetstone, the next valid ley marker is a perfectly straight section of Friern Barnet Lane, where the alignment follows the road towards St. James' Church. This is believed to be part of a very ancient route out of London since Saxon times or before.

St. James' Church Friern Barnet

The history of Friern Barnet is closely linked with the Knights of the Order of St. John of Jerusalem who cared for pilgrims and the sick during the Crusades in the 11th and 12th centuries. In 1199 the Knights were given an estate, approximately where Friary Park is now, and it is possible that they built a hospice near where St. James Church now stands. At this time the main road to the north ran from Muswell Hill down Colney Hatch Lane (then called Halwykstrete) and along Friern Barnet Lane (Wolkstrete) directly past the site of the church.

Opposite the church is the site of the Queen's Well so, as with so many other ancient churches, a holy spring or water source may have been the origin of this sacred place.

At St. James' the road curves around the church, while the ley heads straight for it.

The alignment here runs directly through the west end of the church and through the south door, coincidentally, the oldest part of the building (12th Century).

From the south door, the aligment follows the church path, lined with pollarded yews, then conveniently exits the churchyard through the south gate, as if it had been built for invisible energy streams as much as the church's regular worshippers.

Illustration 39:
St. James' Church Friern Barnet, showing the south door and the path along which the alignment passes.

Illustration 40:
The monument marking the location of the Queen's Well, just a few yards from the church.

Friary Park and the old manor house

800 years ago, Friary Park was a religious establishment owned by the Knights of St John Of Jerusalem. From the 16th Century it has been the site of Friern Barnet's Manor House. When the Friary was demolished workmen claimed to have discovered a tunnel from the house to the church. It followed the same path as the Whetstone Ley and passed beneath the same gateways.

When you walk through the main gate of Friary Park today, you are walking along the alignment (and the course of the tunnel). It follows the path into the park right to the front door of the current Mansion, then through it. Alongside the path, there used to be another stone, remarkably similar to The Whetstone. It was said to be another stepping stone for ladies alighting from coaches or horses. As recently as ten years ago, it was still there, but now seems to have disappeared. Once these things are gone, they're gone for ever.

Illustration 41:
The Whetstone Ley passes directly through the gate of Friary Park, along this path and right through the front door of the old house, site of the ancient Friary.

Numerous other stones, large and small, can be found around the park, in rockeries and in the stream at the bottom of the Park's hill, all possibly remnants of landscaping schemes, perhaps. Take a look and judge for yourself. When I last visited, there was even a new stone circle on the alignment behind the house. A circle of stones around a tree stump. Perhaps the energy of the line itself makes people create these things.

Friary Park's Bringer of Peace

For an supposedy invisible line, at Friern Barnet the Whetstone Ley seems to have a remakable number of things aligned to it. Beyond the old house (site of the Friary and Manor), the alignment is marked by a beautiful monument called The Bringer of Peace. It's a statue, resembling a classical goddess, wielding the sword of truth and justice.

She was erected by Sydney Simmons and dedicated to the memory of Edward VII on 7 May 1910, the day following the King's death. Knowlingly, or otherwise, he erected the monument directly on the Whetstone Ley.

This section of the ley is definitely the most interesting to visit because there is so much to see (and sense). The alignment runs along a length of Friern Barnet Lane, along the paths of St. James's church, through the church gate, across the road through the main gate of Friary Park, along the park path, through the front door of the house, out of a back door and to a statue of a classical goddess figure holding a sword.

It's only a short hop from here up to see the Whetstone, set into the pavement outside The Griffin pub on the High Rd opposite Totteridge Lane.

From there, you could take a tube (nearest station, Totteridge and Whetstone on the Northern Line of the electric worm), or bus, up to High Barnet and visit the ley's terminal point, St. John's Church on Barnet Hill.

Illustration 42:
Friary Park's Bringer of Peace statue, erected directly on the alignment in 1910.

Alexandra Palace

Next notable point on the alignment is Alexandra Palace. For more information on it, refer to page 120 and the Sacred Hills of London Ley. This particular alignment appears to run parrellel to the front of the building crossing the Parliament Hill Ley on the south side. On larger scale maps it can appear to run directly through the rose window, presumably empowering the harmonious influence of its "Earthstar" geometry.

Finsbury Park Hill

Further down the line, we come to another of London's sacred Hills, the one in Finsbury Park. The alignment doesn't hit the summit of the hill, but crosses its southern slopes.

National Maritime Museum

From Finsbury Park the alignment hits a few mark points of lesser importance. The next one worthy of mention is Greenwich Park and the site of the Royal Palace at Greenwich, now the National Maritime Museum and Queens House. This has been a Royal residence since 1427. The Palace of Placentia once stood nearby and was the Birthplace of Henry VIII in 1491.

This area of Greenwich generally has seriously ancient roots. There has been a settlement here since Roman times and on the hill in Greenwich Park is the site of a Roman Temple discovered in1902, not far from Wren's Royal Observatory. I believe the Whetstone Ley extends as far as this hill-top temple.

On the large scale O.S. map, the line can be extended even further, to Chislehurst, site of the mysterious caves with their druid altar and miles of subterranean tunnels. Whether that is a relevant mark point, I don't know.

Chapter Thirteen

The Harestone and Wealdstone Ley

Mark sites

1: St. John The Baptist, Aldenham
2: St. Peter, Bushey Heath
3: The Harestone, Old Redding
4: Brooks Hill and High Street Harrow Weald
5: The Wealdstone
6: Horsenden Hill Greenford
7: Sion House Brentford

Scattered around the London's suburbs are a surprising number of possible megalithic remains, almost all of them linked to leys and alignments.

The Whetstone is prime marker in the previous chapter's ley. The Kingstone, Leytonstone and King Arthur's Stone at St. Pauls all help define the Coronation Line. Whilst over in North West London, we find the Wealdstone, the Harestone, the Headstone and several sarsens beneath Kingsbury Old Church. All of them are on significant ley alignments and several connected in such a meaningful way that it is distinctly possible they are not single, isolated placements. but part of some lost pre-historic grand plan.

Let's first take a look at the Harestone and Wealdstone Ley. This alignment runs approximately 6 degrees west of a N-S orientation - parrallel to the Earthstars N-S axis. To the north, it can be traced back to the old Church of St. John The Baptist, Aldenham. It may extend even further out of London, but for now we will take St. John's as its starting point.

St. John's is a junction point of many other alignments and is a sacred site of indeterminable antiquity. Nobody can be quite certain of the date of Aldenham's first church. However the church's guide itself

146

tells us that the presence of large quantities of Hertfordshire Puddingstone in the current building may indicate that it rests on a site associated with some kind of pre-Christian worship. Parts of the current structure dates from the 12th and 13th century and the East window depicts the 8th Century King Offa holding an Saxon church.

Next point on the alignment is St. Peter's, Bushey Heath, a more recent addition to the landscape. The foundation stone was laid here on 25th August 1836, so ostensibly this does not appear to be an ancient site and there is no mention in the church's history about what was here earlier. Nevertheless, a clue may lie a little way down Elstree Lane in the form of a water pump. Its location in close proximity to the church suggests a source of life-giving holy water at this site.

Third mark point is the mysterious Hare Stone. This stands at the junction of Old Redding and Brook Hill, outside what used to be a pub called The Hare, possibly named after the stone. On my last visit in November 2009, the building was boarded up ready for re-development..

The stone itself is roughly triangular, no more than three or four feet high and is often hidden from view if the shrubbery around it is overgrown. I'm reliably informed that "Harestone" or "Hoarstone" simply means a boundary stone and this location is very close to the old territorial boundary ditches in the grounds of nearby Grimms Dyke Manor.

How old the stone is or what its original purpose was, I do not know and there is very little written about it. Like the Whetstone, it is set at a crossroads and forms part of more than one alignment, linking it to several extremely ancient sites.

From here the ley follows the general direction of Brooks Hill and Harrow Weald High Street. Watkins would have counted these as ley markers.

Next point along the alignment, is the Wealdstone. This nestles beside the kerb outside The Wealdstone Pub at the junction of Wealdstone High Street and College Rd, looking like a beached walrus.

Its a sarsen stone and not from round these parts, so is another piece of our mysterious megalithic heritage and like the Whetstone, sits on one of the lines of the Roman Survey grid discovered by Sir Montague Sharpe.

I noticed that the crossroads here is similar in layout to the one at Whetstone. Not a straight cross, more of a dog's leg junction making the shape of the Sowelo rune of the sun on the landscape, east to west. Was that intentional ? The N-S road through Avebury creates the same shape. Is it significant, or is it just my imagination working overtime?

Next mark point along the ley is Horsenden Hill, Greenford, a magnificent vantage point to look out over the surrounding countryside in any direction. Horsenden Hill is a junction point of a great many leys and, in the Earthstars matrix, is a defining point of two pentagonal star patterns, one huge and covering the whole of Greater London, the other a smaller five-point Earthstar temple centred on St. Mary's at Harrow-on the-Hill (for more information on these, you'll need to see my Earthstars and Visionary Landscape books).

I'm told that once there was evidence of a hill fort at the summit. It was destroyed when the Victorians installed a reservoir beneath the top of the hill. Consequently the Ordnance Survey triangulation point on the hill cannot be taken as an indication of the original highest point here. The whole top of the hill has been flattened artifically. This can be a quite magical place to visit, but take care as some of the wooded slopes of the west side of the hill seem to be a bit of a pervy cruising area.

The last relevant mark point I could find was the grounds of Sion House Brentford, where a rather special 14th century Priory dedicated to St. Bride or Brigit once stood.

Syon Abbey was the only Bridgettine abbey in Medieval England. The abbey belonged to the order established by St Bridget at Vadestena in Sweden in 1346 and was founded in 1415, before moving to Syon from Twickenham in 1431. At the time of the dissolution, the abbey was the 10th richest religious establishment in the country.

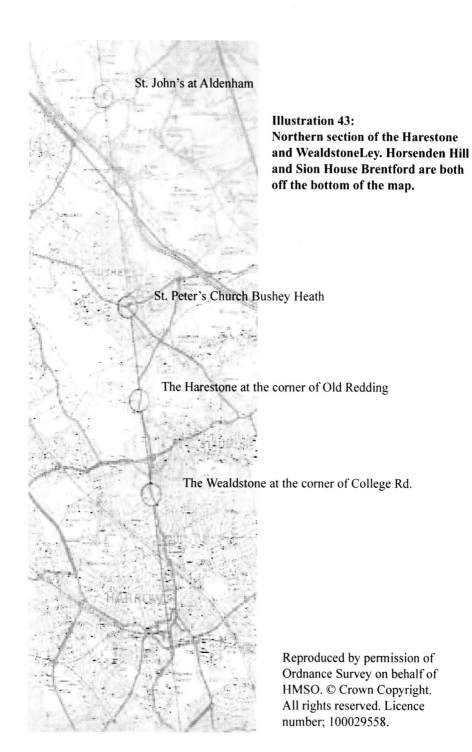

St. John's at Aldenham

Illustration 43:
Northern section of the Harestone
and WealdstoneLey. Horsenden Hill
and Sion House Brentford are both
off the bottom of the map.

St. Peter's Church Bushey Heath

The Harestone at the corner of Old Redding

The Wealdstone at the corner of College Rd.

Illustration 44:
The church of St. John The Baptist at Aldenham, junction point of many alignments, as well as this one.

Illustration 45:
The Harestone at the corner of Old Redding, Harrow, outside what
used to be the Hare pub. On my last visit (Nov 2009) two rectangular
stones had been put next to it.

Illustration 46:
The Wealdstone, at the junction of College Rd and Wealdstone
High street, outside The Wealdstone Pub.

Chapter Fourteen

More Old Stones
The Harestone - Kingsbury Old Church Ley

Mark sites
1: St. Mary's Watford
2: The Harestone
3: Clamp Hill
4: Belmont Hill Stanmore
5: Kingsbury Old Church and sarsen stones

Not only does this alignment feature the Harestone, it contains another four sarsen stones at a remarkable site which confirms that our ancient Parish Churches may have been built on pre-Christian places of worship whose antiquity stretches back into the mists of prehistory; the old church at Kingsbury.

There are actually two churches here, both on the ley. The most noticable is an impressive Victorian structure. It was originally built in Marylebone in 1847 and transported here and re-built stone by stone in 1933.

A few yards away, in an atmospheric wooded corner of the church yard is one of London's hidden gems: the tiny, original 13th Century St. Andrew's Church, the only Grade 1 Listed Building in the Borough of Brent. What makes it particularly interesting is that red Roman tiles can be seen in its walls and the four corners of the church clearly stand on four sarsen stones which may be an indication of an earlier megalithic temple on the site that the church superceded.

This suggestion is suppported by the church's meaningful alignment to another possible megalithic survivor, the Harestone, and to other sites of notable antiquity.

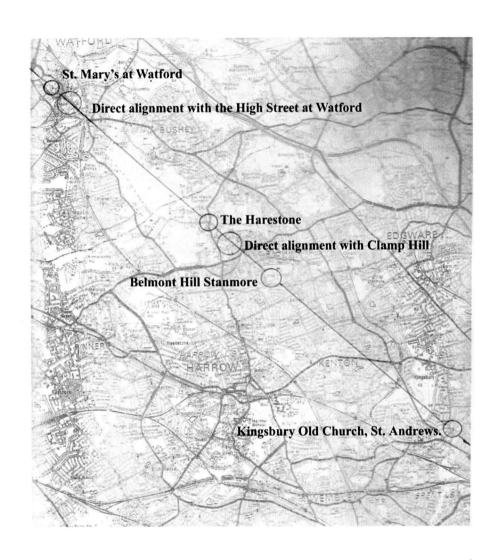

Illustration 47:
The Harestone to Kingsbury Old Church Ley. The alignment passes through old and new St. Andrews' churches at Kingsbury. The old one stands on four sarsen stones.

Illustration 48:
Kingsbury Old Church. Its 13th Century walls, sadly, have been vandalised by garish graffiti. The secluded part of the churchyard that it occupies is unfortunately a magnet for local, bored teenagers and security at the building is poor.

This is a haunting little spot which everyone in London should be made to visit, in order to remind us of the heritage buried beneath our city and its suburbs. It stands amongst a yew grove, and yews are frequently found at ancient Celtic sacred sites. They are the druidic tree of eternal life and re-birth.

Don't ignore the later Victorian church, though. Whoever re-built it here, thoughtfully placed it on the same alignment with the old church and the Harestone, so it benefits from a pleasant energy all of its own.

155

Illustration 49:
Sarsen stones suppport all four corners of old St. Andrew's Church, Kingsbury. Probably part of some earlier megalithic temple at the site and built into the church in this way as part of an attempt to incorporate the earlier religion and its sacred site into the new. Literally.

Illustration 50:
The sarsen stone at the SW corner of Old St. Andrew's Church Kingsbury.

The other four mark points on the alignment are classic ley indicators; the old St. Mary's Church in Watford, the summit of Belmont Hill on Stanmore golf course and the alignment with both Watford High Street and the course of Clamp Hill near the Harestone.

St. Mary's at Watford is one of the largest churches in Hertfordshire and the oldest parts of the building date from 1230. As with most churches of this antiquity, it could mark the site of pre-Christian community celebrations and festivities.

It stands in Watford High Street, within the daunting Watford one - way system, dwarfed by the nearby Harlequin Shopping Centre. Despite these indignities, it still retains an atmosphere of calm and reverence. Interestingly, the alignment runs through the church virtually parrallel to the High Street and the one way system, as if Watford town centre was built around it. Perhaps it was.

Nearer the Harestone, the alignment follows the course of Clamp Hill prefectly. It leads directly towards Belmont Hill which is clearly a solar energy centre on the ley and feels like a very powerful hill-top site. Bel, Baal, Belinus, Beli are all names linked to ancient sun-gods, so this is his "mount".

This notion is reinforced by E. O. Gordon's book, **Prehistoric London**, in which Belmont features as an important location with definite links to many other sites in the capital that would have been significant to our ancestors.

The summit, marked by an Ordnance Survey triangulation point is actually on Stanmore golf course and requires some therapeutic trespassing to reach it. Access is from a narrow path leading up the hill from Mountside and Vernon Drive.

When I visited this spot some years ago, the path was lined with chain link fencing on one side and felt oppressive and confining. I suppose on the positive side, the fence might stop you getting bonked by a stray golf ball.

Chapter Fifteen

The Whetstone to Wealdstone Ley

Mark sites

**1: Church of The Holy Innocents
High Beeches, Epping Forest
2: Bush Hill Park Hill Fort, Enfield
3: The Whetstone
4: St. Joseph's Missionary College Mill Hill
5: Belmont, Stanmore
6: The Wealdstone
7: The possible site of The Headstone
8: Holy Trinity Church Northwood
9: Church at Chalfont St. Peters.**

As proof that these old stones are not scattered about London's suburbs at random, the Whetstone forms part of this lengthy alignment with The Wealdstone.

Synchronistically, it also passes through Headstone Lane where once stood a hefty lump of stone known as the Headstone.

An old postcard dated 1902 shows what may be the Headstone, in the area of Chantry Place at its junction with Headstone Lane. This is nearly 100 yards North of where the alignment passes through, so I can't claim it as a definite mark point on the line, just an interesting curiosity.

Sadly, it seems to have been moved from this location, and no records of its current whereabouts remain, so, it has disappeared with no trace.

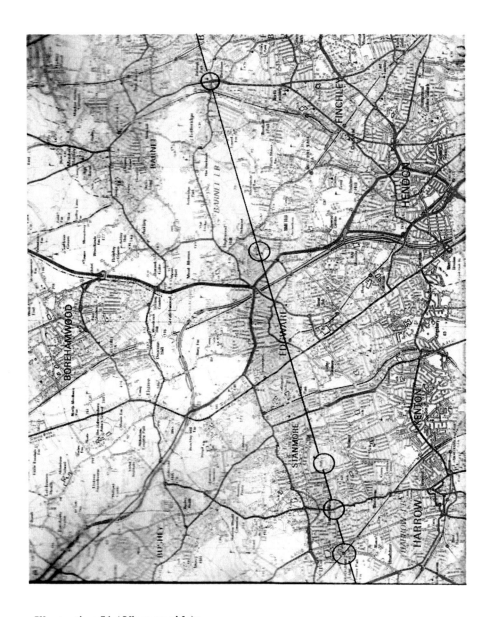

Illustration 51 (View on side):
Part of the Whetstone to Wealdstone Ley

Illustration 52: An old photograph (1902) of the Headstone standing near to Chantry Place. (At the time of writing, this building seems to have been replaced by The Corner Cafe). Whether this was the original location of The Headstone is not known and there is no record of its current whereabouts. My apologies for the poor quality of the photograph (it is very old and faded) and my thanks to Tony Charlton for letting me use it. Without it we'd have no reference of the Headstone at all.

Extending the alignment eastwards provides a connection to another extremely ancient site already mentioned in one of the Sacred Hills of London Leys: the hill fort now forming part of Bush Hill Park Golf Course in Enfield. As mentioned previously, the only remaining banks and mounds are behind the Club House.

Even further East we come to the Church of the Holy Innocents, High Beeches, in Epping Forest.

Its woodland location gives the church a particularly magical atmosphere, but as far as I can tell it is not an ancient site. The present building was built in 1873 to replace an earlier St. Paul's near Lippitts Hill. That was demolished in 1898. No trace of it survives.

St. Joseph's Missionary College Mill Hill

This is a mark point on the alignment between the Whetstone and Belmont Hill Stanmore. It's an impressive building with a huge golden statue of Mary crowning its tower, which can be seen from miles around.

The St Joseph's Foreign Missionary Society was created at Mill Hill in 1866 by Father Herbert Vaughan (1832-1903) and was the first Catholic missionary society to be founded in England.

He probably hadn't a clue that it marked a nodal point in a system of spiritual energy alignments across the capital, but it does. As well as its place in this ley, linking the sites of various megalithic stones, it forms a key part of the complex geometry which is the London Earthstars Landscape Temple. In fact, it is one of the mark sites of the vast 30-point star.

Currently, the building is being re-developed and I am not sure in what form it will survive. It may become a hotel or apartments. We'll have to wait and see. Needless to say, it is not open to the public.

Illustration 53 (above):
The church of The Holy Innocents, High Beeches, Epping Forest.

Illustration 54 (below):
St, Joseph's Missionary College at Mill Hill. The first Catholic Missionary College in England.

To the West, beyond the site of the Headstone, the alignment continues and takes in a further couple of sites; the Church of The Holy Trinity Northwood and the Parish Church at Chalfont St. Peters.

Holy Trinity Northwood is an imposing Victorian Gothic building which looks as if it has stood on this spot since the beginning of time. Surprisingly, it only dates from 1854 when the Parish of Northwood was created (originally the Parish was under the auspices of Ruislip).

I think the Parish church at Chalfont St. Peter is from a similar period, although there is some evidence for an earlier community and sacred spring here.

At the time of the Anglo-Saxon Chronicle in 949, the whole area was known as Ceadeles funtan, which means Caedele's Spring, and rather a plentiful one by the sound of it. Whether that font, fountain or spring was near the present church remains to be seen.

Strict Ley-Hunters would not accept these two churches as genuine ley mark points as their relatively modern status would not contribute to the notion of leys as a provable ancient enigma.

However, those who regard theses alignments as a living and evolving part of the Earth's spiritual dimensions and soul essence, may happily visit such sites and enjoy their inspiration with a clear conscience.

Chapter Sixteen

The Guardian of the Old Stones
and Messenger of the Gods

I was surprised to find how many old stones and prehistoric mounds were scattered around London and its suburbs. A large number of them are listed by Sir Montague Sharpe in his 1919 book, **Middlesex in British, Roman and Saxon Times.**

On page 86, for instance, he informs us that there were ancient stones at the site of Tottenham Cross, at another cross in the Strand (probably the one which stood in the area now occupied by St. Mary-le-Strand), at Stonefield and Stonegrove in Edgware, at Dalston (the Dalstone), at Hoxton (Hochestone), at Haggerston (Hergotstane) at Lisson Grove (Lille Stone), Oswulf's Stone where Marble Arch now stands, the Bordestone at Brentford, the Steyne (stone) at Acton, the Boston (Borderstone) at Boston Manor and at Stone Farm Ealing.

He also mentions the Wealdstone, the Whetstone, the Headstone, the Heathstone and the Sudbury Stone, though mysteriously, not the Harestone, nor the stones beneath Kingsbury Church.

The interesting thing about Sir Montague's book is that he adds to our understanding of these matters considerably. Boundary stones or mark stones, he tells us, were not simply positioned to mark the limits of a plot of land or territory. In Roman times and before, they were held sacred to a minor deity who the Romans called Terminus, the protector of boundaries. His statue was a stone or a post and was often accompanied by a wayside shrine or altar dedicated to other Gods, Goddesses or the Genius Loci of the surrounding fields.

So these things are not mere inanimate rocks, arbitrarily placed to define the limits of a piece of territory. They marked the shrines of the local gods and goddesses and were an important part of the spiritual life of the community. Sir Montague also provides us with an insight into why such items so often stand at a crossroads.

At many crossing points of tracks, he says, were what the Romans called Compita, or as Sir Montague Sharpe refers to them, *"little chapels"* which had *" several sides, each with a doorway and an altar, apparantly for the rites connected with the fertility of several kinds of land holdings in the settlement"*.

I suspect the "many sides' means they were octagonal, and open to the spirits of the eight directions, or "eight winds" an interesting European form of geomancy similar to the eight directions of Feng Shui. Sir Montague informs us that these wayside temples contained shrines to the "Lares" or spirits of the locality.

Elsewhere they are described as towers where *"rustics"* perform sacrifices when the labour of the fields was completed. There are also; *"houses of refreshment for the inhabitants of adjoining lands where little chapels open on all sides are consecrated"*.

So that might explain why mark stones so often stand beside pubs. It is part of the ancient religious customs and a "public house of refreshement" may have been there for as long as the stone.

According to Sir Montague, many of these compita are now the locations of our Parish churches.

"It will be seen from the map, that the sites of over forty seven out of fifty six mother churches of ancient parishes in Middlesex are situated on the quinterial lines defined by the Roman surveyor's landmarks and the inference prima facae is, that such churches occupy the sites of compita or other sacred places existing in Romano British Times."

He then quotes the direction given by Pope Gregory to the

missionary priests being sent to England in order to convert our pagan ancestors. They were under strict instruction to utilise the existing temples of the old religion and re-consecrate them for the new.

This was not new advice. Under an earlier edict in A.D. 392, Theodosius ordered that places of pagan worship were to be used as Christian churches and Honorius in A.D.408 forbade the destruction of pagan edifices. As an example, the Temple of the Pantheon in Rome was turned into a Christian Church dedicated to St. Mary in 508 A.D.

Kingsbury's old church with its four corner stone sarsens and Roman remains clearly visible in its brickwork, now provides an excellent local example.

One of the most important premises of Sir Montague Sharpe's book is that all these significant sites of ceremony or spiritual practice were located in the landscape according to a strictly observed and surveyed Roman grid system.

That may be so, but it is also likely, by their very nature, that these shrines existed prior to the Roman occupation. Many of the descriptions come from Roman times, that is certain, but they are clearly referring, albeit in Roman terms, to practices and places long revered by the local populace. So it can be assumed that our local parish churches stand on some of our earliest sacred sites and places of spiritual experience.

It may be that the Roman concept of the God Terminus had some association with Mercury or Hermes, because in John Michell's ground-breaking work, **The View over Atlantis**, he informs us that *"Hermes is particularly associated with standing stones"* and is *"the Mercurial God of roads and stone pillars"*. So Mercury and Terminus shared some common ground. He continues; *"The Romans found Mercury stones set in lines over the Etruscan countryside. In Greece, the phallic image of Hermes stood in the centre of the market place and the roads that ran in from the surrounding districts were lined with similar stone pillars."*

167

"Watkins compared the straight tracks leading to the Greek cities with the leys of Britain and found in both cases an association with Hermes, known to the Egyptians as Thoth, to the Gauls as Theutates, the name surviving in the numerous Tot or Toot hills all over England. Hermits, he believed, owed their name to their former situation as servants of Hermes, and it does appear that at one time, they acted as guides to pilgrims and travellers across the mountains and wild places."

" All over the world, the ghost of the former mercurial deity hovers above the old paths and standing stones."

In many of these high places, Hermes has now evolved into one of his Christian equivalents, St. Michael or Saint George.

Highgate Hill is a good example of this. The memory of the old Hermitage and Hermit's gate at the summit of the hill is still preserved as the Gatehouse Pub and the parish church dedication is St.Michael.

So it seems the principal guardian of the roads, crossroads and mark stones, in remote antiquity, was a British version of Mercury, Hermes, Theutates or Thoth.

However, he is not alone.

A polarity is at work here and there is a female guardian and goddess of the ways, of equally ancient lineage.

Chapter Seventeen

Our Lady of the Leys
and Barn Hill's Hell's Lane Ley

One of the ideas put forward to explain the function of Leys is the term spirit paths. So what kind of spirits travel these paths ? In Irish legend, our ancestors, the Celts, associated straight ways with paths used by the faeries and other little folk, flying between magical mounds and otherwordly locations.

As we've seen from the last chapter, they also embody a deific energy sometimes perceived as a solar hero or Mercurial spirit, The Quicksilver Messenger.

If these phenomena are linked to the life force of the Earth, then the Earth Spirit herself also exists within the energy presence along these pathways.

In my experience, she often manifests as a "white lady" or Marian apparition, at nodal points along the lines. She's seen by some as a goddess figure akin to Robert Graves' White Goddess, who is the muse, the healer, the inspiration of poets.

To our ancestors, she was known by many names, but one of the clearest descriptions of her comes from the Welsh legends, where she is known as Elen of the Ways, or Sarn Elen, the goddess of paths and trackways.

Elen means bright or shining and is sometimes translated as meaning star. She seems to have been particularly associated with London as a goddess of the city and here she was known by the name of Nehelana, a European version of the Goddess imported from the continent.

The church of Great St. Helen's in the city is probably built upon one of her shrines and in North West London, there is even a rare direct association with one of her ancient paths.

A track running past the foot of Barn Hill in Wembley follows a prehistoric route from the old ford at Westminster up into Hertfordshire and the territories of the Cattuvellaunii tribe who inhabited the area in pre-Roman times.

The path is called Hell's Lane, or in places, Elder Strete. In this instance, the Hell referred to is not the demonic inferno of Christian invention. It comes from Helen or Elen, guardian and bright spirit of the ancient paths. Elder Strete just means old road and may be the origin of the name Elstree which sits on another better-known ancient way, Watling Street.

Elen is said to shine like the sun, indicating that she is a goddess with solar associations, like Brigit, Bride, Sul, Minerva and Athena.

As guardian of the magical pathways of the land, she is surely synonymous with the lines of energy that connect its holy wells, stone circles, sacred hills and other magical or spiritual sites.

It is worth remembering, too, that she is the guardian of inner life paths as well as outer world ones, so at her oracular shrines along the ways of light she may guide you with inspiration, omens, dreams and visions.

Hell's Lane in Wembley is a rare survivor of her paths. Another part is a long straight section of Neasdon Lane that runs all the way down to Duddon Hill, demonstrating how the course of these prehistoric tracks can still be found in modern times.

And, of course, it may be part of a ley, since it aligns to at least a couple of interesting landmarks of special significance.

To the South East, the Barn Hill track forms a direct alignment with the venerable St. Mary's at Willesden Green, former home of a "Black Madonna" with healing powers.

To the North West, it aligns to the lofty summit of Belmont Hill in Stanmore, already a mark point on several other leys.

. If you fancy a woodland walk in the London suburbs, I would recommend a yomp along the wooded Barn Hill section of Hell's Lane, understandably, a more atmospheric and a pleasant experience than the Neasdon Lane section.

Barn Hill itself is worth a visit while you are there. It's a potent junction point of several other leys, one of them an Earthstars line (a 5-point star and midsummer sunrise line) from Horsenden Hill to St. Mary's East Barnet.

You'll find the information board about Barn Hill and Hell's Lane in the car park beside Barn Hill in Fryent Way, Wembley.

Who knows, maybe you'll see or sense Elen herself here on this ancient track. Back in the 80s, at least one person reported seeing an apparition, who they took to be the Virgin Mary, on this ley at Willesden Green's St. Mary's.

I have personally witnessed several "white lady" visitations at various places, most of them old churches dedicated to St. Mary. I believe such sites frequently stand on a very ancient foundation and were probably places where a pre-Christian divine mother was revered.

Remarkably, a number of these St. Mary's churches form a perfectly straight alignment across London which I have rather predictably called London's Mary Line.

That's our next ley.

Illustration 55:
Part of Hell's Lane or Elder Strete, a prehistoric trackway that runs across the
North Eastern base of Barn Hill in Wembley. It takes its name from Elen,
Goddess and Guardian of the ways.

Chapter Eighteen

London's Mary Line

Principal Mark sites

1: **St. Mary le Strand**
3: **St. Mary-le-Bone**
4: **St. Mary Willesden Green where there is a Holy Well and a Black Madonna statue**
5: **St. Mary's Harrow--on-the-Hill**

Additional mark points:
The modern St. Alban's Church in North Harrow
St. Augustine's in Kilburn Park Road
St. Giles-in-the-Fields
plus the site of the Royal Maritime Museum Greenwich, former site of a Royal Palace

Many London alignments have a distinctly feminine presence to their energy. This is one of the most obvious. Its main mark points are a series of very ancient churches, all with a dedication to St. Mary.

In addition, there are a couple of sites which are not St. Mary's, but they are interesting in their own right. St. Giles-in-the-Fields, near the end of Denmark Street and south of New Oxford Street, for instance.

This old church has a very interesting atmosphere, very healing. It was founded in 1101, by Matilda, wife of Henry 1st, as part of a leper hospital and was located in what was then fields, to keep the lepers at a safe distance from normal folk.

Judging by the number of tombs of people who wanted to be

My starting point for this alignment was St. Mary-le-Strand, where this alignment crosses Watkins' Strand Ley. I believe the actual junction is to the West end of the church, in the small garden overlooked by Gibbs' classical temple portico. The atmosphere here always seems soothing and welcoming despite the London traffic hurtling by just feet away.

Stepping into the church through the columns of the ancient temple seems appropriate, for they would form a circle of ten, a decagonal star linked to the Goddess of Love and Heavenly Mother of ancient days.

The church interior is spectacular, particularly the light from the stained glass window. If you find the church open, spend as much time as you can here soaking up the atmosphere.

This may have been the principal sacred site within the old Saxon settlement of London, the Ald Wych.

A holy well was nearby, as was a venerated stone cross and London's most popular maypole.

More information on St. Mary-le-Strand can be found in the Strand Ley section.

Next St. Mary along the line is Marylebone.

St. Mary-le-Bone

The current church on Marylebone Road is the fourth to serve this parish. The first was actually the parish church of Tyburn. It was built around 1200, dedicated to St. John the Evangelist and stood quite a distance away in the vicinity of the present Marble Arch, where Sir Montague Sharp locates Oswulf's Stone.

Around 1400, the first St. Mary's was built, not far away from the present church. A small memorial garden at the North end of

Marylebone High Street marks its original location and I believe this alignment passes through parts of both the 15th Century site and the present one.

The original dedication of the church was to St. Mary the Virgin by the Bourne; a reference to the Ty Bourne, a stream that used to run from what is now Regent's Park down to the Thames.

In time, the dedication became St Mary-le-Burn, then Marylebone. We can still see what the interior of the original church looked like since it is portrayed by the artist Hogarth (1697-1764) in the marriage scene from his famous series "The Rake's Progress" (1735).

The great Elizabethan philosopher Francis Bacon (1561-1626) was married in the old church in 1606.

The modern church is well worth spending time in. The gardens to the east of the church have a circle of benches around a wonderful old tree and provide a perfect spot for outdoor meditation. There is also an excellent crypt cafe.

St. Augustine's Church, Kilburn Park Rd

According to one web site, St Augustine's is one of the most breathtaking Victorian churches in the whole of England, a fusion of French-inspired detailing and Anglo-Catholic tradition, with a soaring 254ft. steeple that wasn't completed until 20 years after the body of the church was finished in 1877.

What is more important, possibly, is that St. Augustine's is believed to stand close to the original site of Kilburn Priory, an important religious establishment founded in the 12th century.

To prove it, just around the corner in Coventry Close, opposite the Bell Inn, are some actual physical remains of the priory, including several massive lumps of masonry and a deep well.

The Bell Inn is thought to have stood on an ancient place of refreshment associated with the Holy Well of Kilburn, the Wells Tea House, which along with the well itself, was visited by many travellers on the ancient pilgrim route to St. Alban's (now Edgware Rd).

So the well in Coventry Close is a Holy Well deserving of some honour and pride.The current impression it gives is that it has been abandoned and forgotten. If you decide to visit the spot, give the well a blessing and invoke the return of the grail maiden of its sacred waters. She is still there on the inner planes.

The priory, like so many others, came to an end with the dissolution of the monasteries under Henry VIII and it is assumed these few remnants have lain here for nearly five hundred years, while the stones that formed the rest of the priory were carted off to be used in other buildings.

So, although St. Augustine's is a relatively recent addition to the landscape, it stands near a sacred site of immense antiquity.

It is worth noting, too, that in keeping with the spirit of this alignment, the dedication of Kilburn Priory was originally to the Blessed Virgin Mary though it was shared with St. John the Evangelist.

The Shrine of Our Lady of Willesden

Next point along the line is the "Parish Church of Willesden Green and Shrine of Our Lady," Our Lady in this case being Mary Magdalene.

This is another of London's hidden gems. You'll find it five minutes walk down Neasden Lane from Neasden tube station. Parking is near impossible, so the best alternative to the tube is to parachute in.

The area itself has not benefitted from inspired development so

St. Mary's stands as a spiritual oasis amid many less marvellous surroundings. In fact, it has stood here since the year 938 when this was open pastures. The church proudly boasts it is home to the ancient shrine of Our Lady of Willesden, and to the Holy Water of Willesden which flows underneath the building.

Normally a Marian shrine grows up around the site of a vision of "Our Lady" as at Walsingham or Lourdes. In the 80s, local newspapers did carry reports of someone witnessing an apparition of the Blessed Virgin here. Sadly though, any earlier visions associated with the shrine's origins are now forgotten and lost in time.

Its a safe bet that whatever marked this place as a sacred site was focussed around the healing waters of the Holy Well. The name Willesden is recorded as Welles Dun in the Domesday Book. It means the hill of wells (or possible the well beneath the hill).

Certainly her sacred waters still flow beneath the church and surface in what is now the boiler room. Since that isn't exactly convenient for visitors, some thoughtful pipework leads it up into the knave where a standpipe can be used by modern-day pilgrims to fill bottles.

The water is believed to have healing properties, particularly for eye problems. On my last visit, the caretaker said that he tries to open the church every day, except Tuesday, for people to visit, pray, meditate and take the waters.

In the 15th and 16th Centuries, the Shrine was at the height of its popularity, counting Thomas Moore amongst its visitors. However, its venerated statue of the Black Madonna was removed by Cromwell in 1538. I have been told that it was cast into the vicarage pond, but other records suggest it was taken to Cromwell's house in London where she was burnt, like a witch, along with several other similar Marian figures. Not a nice man, Cromwell.

Over 400 years passed before a replacement was commisioned in 1972 and, carved from a local oak, it now stands proudly inside the church, as a reminder of the shrine's origins and history. The interior of the church carries a very uplifting energy and presence and is always surprisingly warm and welcoming.

St. Mary The Virgin Harrow-on-the-Hill

St. Mary's at Harrow is one of the most important sacred sites within the whole London area. It dominates the skyline from many of London's holy hills and other sacred places.

Its sense of numinous power marks it as either the end or start point of this alignment and it is demonstrably a junction of a great many others.

As a sacred site it is incalculably ancient. The first church here is recorded as having been founded in 1094 by Bishop Lanfranc. However, the wooded area next to the church and known as The Grove suggests far older connections.

The name of "The Grove" hints at a druid site. Earthworks within the area could be the remains of the ramparts of a hill fort and the fishponds on the hillside near the earthworks are referred to in a document dated 1554 as "Harrow Well", so there may have been a sacred well or spring here, just as there were holy waters at St. Mary-le-Strand's well, St. Mary-le-Bone's Ty Bourne and Willesden's Holy Well.

Mary does seem to be connected to the "Waters of Life" both literally and figuratively, as the life force flowing within these alignments.

The most interesting fact about St. Mary-on-the-Hill at Harrow, though, is its parallels with the mysteries of Rennes le Chateau in SW France.

No, I don't mean that the vicar of St. Mary's has suddenly and mysteriously acquired a treasure, like Berenger Sauniere, the priest of

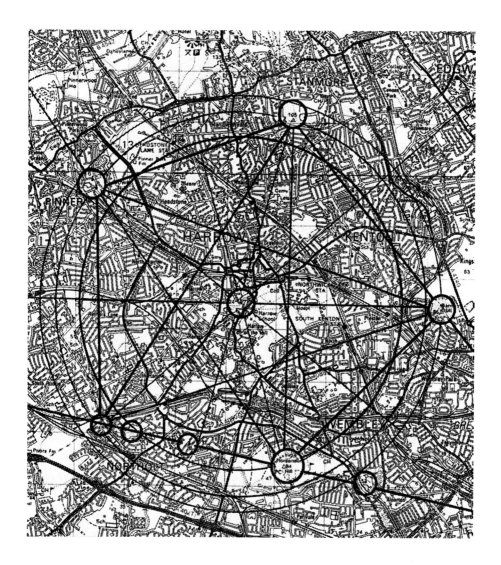

Illustration 56:
The Earthstars Pentagram of sites, mostly hilltops, centred on St. Mary's Church at Harrow-on-the-Hill. This connects to the larger five-point star of the London Earthstars geometry and if you re-create it on your own O.S. maps, you will find its individual alignments connect up to many other significant sacred sites all over London and its suburbs.

179

Rennes-le-Chateau who appeared to have come into millions overnight. I am referring to the fact that Rennes Le Chateau's St. Mary's sits at the centre of a perfect pentagram of five hills, well documented by Henry Lincoln (co-author of The Holy Blood and Holy Grail) in his books on the subject, the last one being **The Holy Place**.

Remarkably, the church of St. Mary the Virgin atop the hill at Harrow forms the centre point of a similar pentagonal landscape temple. Many of the sites defining this geometry will be familiar, since several of them have cropped up on leys we have already featured.

The five star-points are Horsenden Hill Greenford, Barn Hill Wembley, Belmont Hill Stanmore, Dabbs Hill Northolt and St. John's Pinner. The pentagram itself is slightly irregular, because although the five points are set precisely at the pentagonal angle of 72 degrees around St. Mary's, they are not all at the same distance from the centre. This does not undermine the validity of the figure, the rarity of such an occurance or its importance. The geometry and alignments they create are extremely significant.

The line from Horsenden Hill to Barn Hill is a midsummer sunrise alignment which continues to St. Mary's East Barnet and forms the side of a large (16.2 miles diameter) pentagon in the London Earthstars' geometry.

Horsenden Hill itself is the NW point of that larger 5 point star around London and the line from the Dabbs Hill to Horsenden Hill is also part of the Earthstars geometry. It can be continued into central London as a main axis of the larger pentagram, passing through One Tree Hill Alperton, St. Dunstan's-in-the-west Fleet Street, St, Bride's Fleet Street, the London Stone and Tower Hill.

In the opposite direction it links to St. Mary's Denham, St. James at Gerrard's Cross and to Bulstrode Camp. Draw this geometry upon your own O.S.map and you will find that many other lines extend to significant ancient sites all over the London suburbs.

This kind of evidence moves leys from a simple linear phenomena which could have been contrived by early humanity, to a global grid built upon the planetary web of life. Pentagonal patterns such as this are part of the Rose Grids linked to the feminine life force of our Earth. The larger Earthstars are referred to in the Hopi Prophesy as the "Great Driver Wheels."

It also demonstrates that sacred sites should never be viewed in isolation. They were always seen in context of the whole, as part of a ritual and sacred landscape involving many other sites to which they connect and relate in ways we have long forgotten.

Here, the Harrow pentagram creates a sacred landscape that covers a large area of North West London, but its importance and its extended alignments also make it part of the larger sacred landscape of Greater London, whose alignments, in turn, connect to other sites the length and breadth of the land.

Such patterns create a power and presence in places that can far exceed the usual experience of its individual sanctuaries or shrines.

This is because the place is more strongly connected to the universal and planetary energies than one would at first suspect.

All things are connected.

The Harrow pentagram's mark points are close enough to allow a pilgrimage to all of them on the same day.

Try it. You'll be surprised how prominently Harrow-on-the-Hill and its church spire stand out and dominate the skyline from many of these sites, allowing you to anchor the energy back to the centre from the points of the star temple.

This is also a good place to experiment with sacred sound and its effects on the energies of place. A CD of sacred music (Benedictine chant perhaps), played at all six points (including the centre) simulta-

-neously, might generate an interesting and beneficial change in the atmosphere and serve to help re-build the pathways of subtle forces between these sites.

The late Colin Bloy, who combined dowsing with his skills as a healer, maintained that you could play a recording of a Benedictine Chant in the centre of an empty field and that within 20 minutes it will have generated the energy pattern of the Cathedral where it was recorded.

The harmonies of sacred geometry and sacred sound are inter-related. Music is harmony in time. Geometry is harmony is space.

Finally, I think it worth mentioning that the pentagram is not a sinister symbol, associated exclusively with satanic and witchy pursuits in second-rate horror movies and uninformed minds.

It was originally the emblem of the Pythagorean Mystery School and was considered a symbol of good fortune, good health and protection.

This is because it embodies the mathematical principle of the Golden Mean, the law of proportion deemed to represent and create beauty and harmony throughout nature.

It is also associated with the goddess of love and planet Venus whose journey through the heavens blazes a vast five-point star in the night sky over an eight year period.

Such a pattern, overlaid as a temple groundplan upon any landscape can only be a very beneficial influence upon the territory it covers. It marks a plot, in this case a quite large one, of sacred ground.

I know that will be hard to believe for those who are familiar with some of the less attractive parts of North West London, but we are dealing here with a construction of the often-disregarded spiritual dimensions of our environment, not just the reality of the material world.

Chapter Nineteen

The London Stone Ley

Original mark points

St. Martin's Ludgate
St. Paul's Cathedral
The London Stone in Cannon Street
All Hallows-by-the-Tower
The Tower of London

Additional mark points

St. Mary's Willesden Green
The former Holy Trinity Church opposite Great
Portland Street tube
The Chapel of Lincoln's Inn Fields

This is a slightly controversial alignment, based on a five point ley first mentioned in **The Ley Hunters' Guide** written by Ian Thompson and Paul Devereux, the former editor of **The Ley Hunter Magazine** and renowned authority on these matters. The five points were St. Martin's Ludgate Hill, St. Paul's Cathedral (the alignment barely clips the SW corner, but this would have been part of the older Cathedral destroyed in the Great Fire), All Hallows-by-the-Tower and the North side of the Tower of London.

I have extended it to take in a few more mark sites. To the North West it aligns to the lovely old St. Mary's at Willesden Green, with its Holy Well and Black Madonna.

On the way, it takes in the former Holy Trinity Church opposite Great Portland Street tube station and the chapel of Lincoln's Inn Fields. Strictly speaking, neither would have been old enough to qualify as a valid ley marker using the parameters laid down by Thomspon and Devereux at that time.

But as I've said before, I believe leys are not simply a remnant of a long forgotten science or art, but a living, evolving part of the Earth's life force, so if they are also marked by appropriate places that are not-so-old, it is quite acceptable to my line of thinking.

Having said that, I have to admit that the key point in this line is said to be of considerable antiquity and importance; the London Stone.

This is reputed to be the legendary foundation stone of the city or of its principle temple to Diana Artemis set up by Brutus the Trojan, grandson of Aeneas, when he settled here around 1100 B.C.

The tale is recorded in the works of Nennius and Sir Geoffrey of Monmouth. Now regarded as myth, if remembered at all, it was accepted as fact until the mid 19th century.

The **Agas Map of London**, dated 1633, states unreservedly that London was founded by Brutus as "New Troy" some 1,130 years before the birth of Christ.

"This ancient and famous city of London was first founded by Brute the Trojan, in the year of the world, two thousand, eight hundred, thirty and two, before the nativity of our Saviour Christ, one thousand one hundred and thirty. So that since the first building it is two thousand seven hundred and sixty and three years. And afterwards repaired and enlarged by King Lud. "

Historians, if they are aware of the story at all, tend to dismiss it as fiction rather than fact. As Tolkien observed, history at its most ancient first evolves from fact into legend, then into myth.

Whether the story is true or not, the fact that it exists at all should make The London Stone a treasured piece of London's heritage proudly displayed at some focal point in the city. After all, it could be the oldest relic of our capital.

But no. Sadly, its possible importance has been overlooked and unacknowledged for many years.

Some of the blame for this lies at the feet of the historian Camden, who dismissed the stone as a Roman Milestone. It was, he suggested, a Millarium, marking the central point of the city from which all distances were measured. Because he is a credible source, his opinion is accepted and often repeated despite the fact that there is no record whatsoever of the London Stone in Roman times and no other supporting evidence.

The earliest written mention of it is from the 10th Century, according to the 16th Century historian John Stowe. He found references from the time of Athelstane which list lands and property as being *"near unto London Stone"*. Writing about the Stone in 1598, he describes it as follows:

"Standing in Walbrook, on the south side of this High Street, neere unto the channel, is pitched upright a great stone called London Stone, fixed in the ground very deep, fastened with bars of iron, and otherwise so stronglie set that if cartes do runne against it through negligence, the wheeles be broken, and the stone itself unshaken. The cause why this stone was there set, the verie time when or other memorie thereof, there is none."

Sounds like a sizeable megalith. the London Stone we are left with these days is no more than three feet by two and so must be a mere remnant of the original.

There are many beliefs attached to the stone. E.O. Gordon, the author of **Prehistoric London**, believed that the stone was an important outlying marker related to the stone circle formerly on Ludgate Hill.

185

She also held the opinion, as I do, that this could have been the stone from which King Arthur pulled his sword of sovereignty (see my book **London's Camelot and the Secrets of the Grail** for my full explanation of this) and that it had been moved from an original location close to St. Paul's.

Folklore decrees that the safety of the city is inextricably entwined with the safety of the stone. An ancient proverb tells us: *'So long as the stone of Brutus is safe, so long shall London flourish.'* Presumably that is why it is housed in a protective stone surround behind an iron grill. You can hardly see it.

For centuries, the London Stone stood prominently in the very centre of Cannon Street until it became a nuisance to horse-drawn traffic. It was moved to the nearby churchyard of St. Swithins in 1742.

When the church was demolished as part of a redevelopment scheme in 1972, the stone's fame had faded and it was set into the wall of the Overseas Banking Corporation of China at 111 Cannon Street where it remains to this day.

The Chinese Bank has now closed and the future of the stone is under the aegis of the site's developers (Minerva PLC) who say it will be suitably rehoused within any new development and safely removed to the Museum of London during any demolition of the building.

The London Stone is an incredibly important part of the City's heritage. So it is no wonder that its alignment connects to other important locations, like St. Paul's Cathedral and the Tower of London.

It could however be on a more important alignment. While checking the long distance connections of this one, I found that by altering its course slightly, it could target some more significant sites.

Using a 1:50,000 Ordnance Survey map, I found that if I lined up the London Stone to the White Tower, the alignment passes through the main body of St. Paul's rather than skimming a corner.

The White Tower is arguably the most important site within the Tower of London precincts. According to E.O. Gordon's **Prehistoric London**, it was built upon the site of a chalk-lined mound know as the Bryn Gwyn (the white mount) which was the reputed burial place of Bran the Blessed and Brutus himself, so the new slant on the alignment gains some status and a stronger connection to the city's legendary founder.

In the process, the line loses St. Martin's at Ludgate and All Hallows by the Tower as markers. On the plus side, it gains two old St. Marys. St. Mary-at-Hill and St. Mary's at Harrow-on-the-Hill.

It also acquires a puzzling collection of stones as mark point in Wapping.

The recreation ground beside Greenbank E1 and Tench Street contains over thirty huge stones. By no stretch of the imagination has anyone tried to use them as a landscaping project. They look as if they have been simply tipped off the back of a lorry and left there. There's enough to make two or three good sized stone circles, but whether they are the remains of an ancient monument is debatable. They might just be the Parks Department's idea of a rockery.

It just struck me as rather synchronistic that they line up so well with a series of London's most ancient sites, the Bryn Gwyn (White Tower), the London Stone, St. Paul's (possible location of a stone circle) and St. Mary's at Harrow.

Maybe they are just another example of how appropriate things tend to end up on these lines.

If anyone has any contact with Tower Hamlets Parks' Department, see if you can get them to re-position the stones as a proper modern circle.

Illustration 57 and 58:
The Wapping Stones. The largest one (top photo) looks like a skull. They don't
seem to be old. No mention of them on early maps. So is this a very syncronistic
placing on an appropriate alignment ?

Main mark points on the alternative London Stone Ley;

1: The Wapping Stones
2: The Tower of London
3: The White Tower, site of the Bryn Gwynn "White Mount"
4: St. Mary-at-Hill
5: The London Stone
6: St. Paul's Cathedral
7: The centre of the Inner Circle, Regents Park
8: Harrow School
9: St. Mary's, Harrow-on-the-Hill

Chapter Twenty

The Penton Ley

Main Mark points

1: Willesden Green Holy Well
2: St, Andrew's Church in Willesdon High Street
3: The Sacred Heart of Jesus Church in Quex Rd, NW6
4: St. Mary-in-the-Fields, Abbey Rd, NW6
5: Site of Barrow Hill Mound beside Primrose Hill
6: The Penton, site of ziggurat-style, stepped pyramid mound, demolished by the Victorians to create a reservoir
7: Site of Merlin's cave beneath the Penton mound
8: St. Leonard's Shoreditch
9: Alignment corresponds to the orientation of Calvert Ave and Rochelle Street right through Arnold Circus mound
10: Arnold Circus mound, associated with a much visited shrine to "Our Lady" like Willesden Green Church
9: St. Matthew's, the Mother Church of Bethnal Green
10: Church of the Ascension, Baxter Road, Custom House

This is a lengthy alignment marked principally by a succession of sites of accepted antiquity, including three ancient mounds and five wells or springs, plus a handful of interesting spots with a charm of their own.

It begins at the remarkable Shrine of Our Lady of Willesden Green with its Holy Well and Black Madonna.

Next point is St. Andrew's Parish Church in Willesden High

Street, an impressive building dating from 1887, but not as far as we know, built upon an older site.

Next spot is the Sacred Heart of Jesus Church (and possibly the Methodist Church nearby) in Quex Rd West Hampstead. Both stand on land previously thought to have been owned by the nuns of Kilburn Priory.

Just around the corner in Abbey Rd, is the next site, the neo-gothic St. Mary's-in-the-Fields Kilburn. It is no longer in the fields, but presumably was when it was first built in 1856 and like many of the other churches in this locality, it claims to have been built close to the site of Kilburn Priory or Abbey.

The next point is at Primrose Hill, but is not the hill itself. It is the site of a barrow (still marked as Barrow Hill on some maps) which once stood on the side of Primrose Hill.

Sadly the barrow no longer exists, having been replaced by an underground reservoir in Victorian times, so we can safely assume it had a free flowing spring beneath it.

Next point on the line is also now a reservoir, but before the Victorian Era, was a stepped pyramid mound known as The Pen Ton, which translates as the Hill of the Head (E. O. Gordon's **Prehistoric London**).

Beneath it, legend insists was Merlin's Cave. A local pub of the same name is believed to had access to the cave through its cellars in the last century and opened it as a tourist attraction. If the cave still exists, the entrance into it from the pub may provide access again at some time in the future.

Moving on down the alignment, we find ourselves at St. Lawrence's Church Shoreditch. A water pump to the north of the church suggests more holy waters beneath the ground, which wouldn't be surprising as Holy Well Priory was just down the road.

191

The first recorded church here dates from 1160 and of course, it stands on Ermine Street at the junction of two other Roman Roads, so may claim origins as a wayside shrine similar to those described by Sir Montague Sharpe.

I personally find the atmosphere here a bit unsettling, but haven't fathomed why as yet.

Alongside the church runs Calvert Way, roughly in the same orientation as the alignment. It leads directly to Arnold Circus Mound, which you may remember from the Coronation Line and Watkins' Strand Ley.

As we learned back then, it was associated with a nearby "Monkish establishment" where a wooden statue of The Virgin Mary was reputed to possess healing powers.

Possibly that was the nearby Priory of St. Mary, Spitalfields which stood a little way to the South, while the Priory of St. John The Baptist, Holywell, stood a short distance to the west.

This may be the end point of the alignment as the two remaining sites are relatively modern.

The first is St. Matthew's, the Mother Church of Bethnal Green, built in the 18th century by Charles Dance.

Last point (as far as I know) is The Ascension Church in Baxter Road, Custom House, dating from 1903 and still serving as a church and community centre.

The End of The Lines

That brings us to the end of the section on alignments.

Obviously, the Greater London area contains far more leys than I have listed here. I've just highlighted the ones I thought were the most interesting or important.

There are lots more. I have maps covered in a mind-boggling scrawl of lines. Some valid. Some speculative. Some totally meaning-less.

Whatever their merits, they will have to wait for a follow-up second (or third) volume before they are exposed to public scrutiny.

This is where you could help. If you have plotted an outstanding alignment in your area, start compiling details of its defining sites and anything else notable along the line. Make a map or diagram and email some preliminary details to Earthstars Publishing. Write up your own chapter on the ley if you want.

Chances are, we'll have enough to fill another book in no time and if we use your material, you'll get a full credit.

It'll take a while to get published, of course. The research on this one has been collected over many years and it has taken at least four years to write up and produce.

With a bit of luck and more people contributing, volume two will not take so long.

Chapter Twenty One

This Way Lies Madness
- a cautionary note

When you develop an interest in leys, there are two things you will definitely need, and they are not necessarily a map and a ruler. First and foremost, you should be equipped with a thick skin and a sense of humour.

This is because the subject is an easy target for the cynical, the skeptical and the shallow opportunistic comedian. Some of your oldest and closest friends, if you tell them what you are doing, will assume that somewhere down the ley line you have lost your marbles. To these people, the adjective that derives from the noun ley is 'do-lally'.

This reaction most often comes from the uninformed, who know little about the subject. Yet it can also represent the attitude of the academically inclined, and otherwise knowledgeable, who will tell you that the case for leys is not scientifically proven and to put it bluntly, they don't exist. In academic circles, the subject of leys lies behind a very firmly closed door, along with other things too cranky to contemplate.

As I said in the opening chapter, leys maybe compared to the hidden knowledge of a secret tradition.

To those in the know, like many of the mysteries of nature, they are an open secret, on public display, for anyone willing to investigate and decipher their enigmas. Their many incomprehensible elements are part of their magic, mystery and allure.

By contrast, to the uninitiated and uncomprehending, they are as elusive as a beam of starlight and equally intangible. Like fairies, if you don't believe in them, they aren't there.

So should every ley map carry the legend and warning: "This way lies madness"?

Possibly. After all, you will be visiting places where humanity traditionally interacts with our divine spiritual dimensions and where, according to Dr. James Swan and other researchers, people may hear voices, see visions, experience altered states of consciousness, enjoy feelings of euphoria, be suddenly and miraculously healed, encounter telepathic animals or inexplicable energies.

It's understandable why some of these things may give cause for concern regarding one's mental stability.

Fortunately, they are more to do with the place than your state of mind. It comes with the territory.

In my opinion, the kind of people who do actually experience any of these things, are mostly delighted by the occurrence and are far from barmy.

At worst, they might be evolving a rather rewarding kind of nuttiness in keeping with the best traditions of British eccentricity and the ways of the visionary, the artist and poet.

The mysteries of the Earth are the mysteries of life itself and much knowledge and wisdom is encoded in our ancient sacred sites and spiritual visionary landscape.

If there is any madness attached to it, it is the kind that makes you feel suddenly inspired and full of ideas when you sit in a particular place, perhaps by a tree, a well or spring.

The kind of madness that miraculously attracts pilgrims to

Lourdes and other holy shrines, with a promise to cure the incurable.

The kind of madness that leads you to the realization that the world all around you possesses life and consciousness of its own and can even communicate with you, in strange and unusual ways.

Or the kind of madness that tells you that you belong here, you are part of the whole, that all things are connected, in many incomprehensible ways, and we are all one.

Compared to the madness that passes for normal life in the shallow, agnostic materialistic worlds of commerce, finance and politics, it's remarkably sane.

What is important is your personal experience. That alone will convince you whether there is some special numinous quality operating at the sites which define leys, or some revelatory power that inspires and enlightens.

So drag yourself out of that comfy chair, switch off the TV, put on some good walking shoes and get out there into the real world.

The X files was right on one thing.

The truth is out there.

Scully off and find it.

Chapter Twenty Two

Walking The Line

As the title suggests, this is the part of the book where we elicit your involvement and suggest you put this notion about paths of enlightenment to the test, rediscover the art of pilgrimage, step boldy into the visionary landscape and see what you find.

There are two basic elements to consider: lines and sites. Which is more important? Personally, I regard the defining sites as more significant and interesting than the alignments, simply because they are often points where more than one ley crosses. As a result, they can usually appear to be more potent places of power.

They are also frequently locations where a powerful vertical shaft of the universal life force interacts with the ley network. That's what really makes these places power points. It's not a two dimensional thing. It's multi-dimensional.

Earth energies are part of the universal life force, as well as the planetary life force. These are places where we can plug ourselves into the cosmic mains.

That said, don't ignore the lines. Walk them where you can and along the way, look for any evidence of their parallel reality.

If you know you are actually on a ley, can you feel anything, any flow of energy? Does it have a direction? Where do you feel it? What does it feel like? How wide is the line?

Look for gates and paths positioned along the course of the ley, like those at St. James' in Friern Barnet.

If you are into dowsing, get your pendulum or rods out. I am not going to attempt to condense the vast subject of dowsing into a couple of inadequate paragraphs here. If you want to pursue that line of business, visit the website of the renowned dowser Hamish Miller and buy his Wee Book on Dowsing (www.hamishermiller.co.uk). That will tell you all you need to know. Alternatively, you could take a look at the British Society of Dowser's website (www.britishdowsers.org) .

Once you start dabbling with leys, you may find yourself drawn to your local sacred sites. Go with the flow and visit them. It doesn't matter if you don't know how they connect or if they are on any leys. You'll get to know soon enough, if they are.

In London, you can investigate the sites in this book, or visit the Earthstars sites, some of which are listed on the earthstars.co.uk web site.

Things to do on a ley pilgrimage

People often ask what's the best thing to do at these places to interact with the spirit of place. There are many possible answers. The simplest is do nothing. As it says in Chapter One of **Earthstars The Visionary Landscape**:

> *" The Earth speaks to us.*
> *You just need to find the right place to sit still and listen."*

Chill out. Relax. Take long, slow, deep breaths. Drift into a daydream. Meditate, in any way you're used to. Still the active mind. Let the atmosphere and energy of the place seep into you. Have no expectations. Just see what comes. It might be nothing, but be positive, take a notepad.

There's a lot more you could do, and we'll come to those things later, but sitting quietly and being open to inspiration is the basic starting point.

While you are walking around, taking in first impressions, there are a few things to consider.

One simple way to initiate an interaction with the spirit of place is to verbally or telepathically greet and bless the site when you arrive (some suggested blessings are included at the end of this chapter).

If you want to be more thorough, bless and honour the spirits of the place, the gods, goddesses or guardians of the site and the ancestors who previously revered it and sought sanctity here for many centuries.

If it is a church or cathedral, look at the structure of the building. The renowned dowser and healer, Colin Bloy, founder of the Fountain International community healing project (fountain-international. org), claimed that many churches, abbeys and cathedrals were designed in accordance with a system aligning them to the human chakras.

In practice, this means the length of a church's nave may be divided by a series of pillars and arches creating seven bays each relative to the seven human chakras.

Furthest away from the altar is the base chakra, whilst the apse will be the focus of the third eye/brow and crown chakras. The pulpit will invariably be close to the throat chakra.

Mystics suggest the system may symbolise the body of Christ, or the supreme deity within whom we live, breath and have our being. Others claim it simply represents the invisible spirit within matter. Both seem valid perspectives.

If you have a strong affinity to this system, you can sometimes feel a distinct reaction in the region of your own chakras as you walk the length of a church or cathedral, down the central aisle.

In my experience, you will feel these sensations most strongly around the altar where the energy can be more intense. You may feel sensations in your head, brow or crown, or even hear a high-pitched hum or whistle of the energy. Don't imagine you've developed tinnitus. It's the energy of the leys and will miraculously fade and stop depending on your location.

Some dowsers maintain that there is always a ley running down the centre aisle of old churches and that it invariably crosses with other leys at the altar. As you might remember, a couple of the Watkins Leys conform to this, with the ley running right down the centre of the church. But equally, some don't. I find it hard to believe this could be the case in every church, but you never know. See what you find personally.

Another thing to look out for is the sense that you have stepped into a column of light and energy. These are vertical components of the ley system. It is a multi- dimensional grid with connections off-planet and to the heart of the Earth's inner core. The life force of the Earth is an intrinsic component of the Universal Life Force.

We, of course, are an intrinsic part of both, on a level that probably can't be proven scientifically until someone invents a device for detecting and measuring the human soul. But that's why we can interact with these energies consciously.

These are our soul lines. We are born to Earth through them and leave again on our deaths to travel back to the stars. So it is appropriate that births and deaths are celebrated at these sacred centres.

Holy Hills

Hills seem to have their own natural chakras which can be felt as you climb to the summit. Perhaps that's why high places are traditionally dwelling places of the gods and recognized as sacred.

I first noticed this at Primrose Hill some years back. Approaching the hill from the southern side, I felt an energy sensation in my base chakra. As I walked up the path to the top, the sensation rose up my body through my chakras, until at the crown of the hill, it was buzzing quite noticeably at my crown. It was a good lesson in why there may be more to the idea of sacred hills than just terminology.

Those who are aware of the process are open to divine inspiration and other experiences when they reach the summit of the hill. In my case, there was a surprising vision of an angelic or devic being, who overlights the place.

Walking up the northern slope of the hill, prompted a completely different experience, so the phenomenon may be dependant on which direction you approach the summit.

You may notice this effect on any of London's other hills. Many of them certainly have a sense of being places of great power.

Spheres of influence

All sacred sites have a sphere of influence, like an energy dome, or force field, around and above the place.

Think of it as an aura of energy surrounding the heart of the site. It will have several concentric rings to it and some starbursts of sacred geometry within them, so when approaching an energy centre, try to sense where you pass through the various layers of its auric bubble.

With particularly powerful sites, the sphere of influence can reach many miles to interact with other energy centres.

For instance, the sphere of influence of St. Mary's in East Barnet, or St. Mary's at Harrow-on-the-Hill extends to many other sites in their areas and beyond, whether they are linked by straight line leys or not. Sometimes spheres of influence interact forming connections of sacred geometry.

On your journey along the paths of enlightenment, you'll find that quite a lot of other things have a sphere of influence, as a kind of extended aura.

Trees, standing stones, wells, springs, all have their own subtle energy and you can learn to sense it with practice.

A basic exercise to try with a tree or standing stone, is to locate a point where you can start to feel the energy around it, then move closer, or back away, while you try to sense changes in its layers of energy. You should be able to detect several distinct points where the energy in the sphere of influence changes.

The song of the Earth

I've found that some old churches have such harmony built into their architecture that the building literally sings and, in turn, singing, toning or chanting in them has the power to energise the place and the leys that radiate from it.

St. Dunstan's-in-the-West, in Fleet Street, falls into this category. It's an octagonal church with amazing acoustic resonance.

Music in general can empower the connections of our sacred landscape.

I realized this as I walked back to work from lunch one day. I was strolling up Southampton Row towards Euston Road, when I felt as if I had stepped into a massive wall of energy.

As I reached St. Pancras Church on the corner of Euston Road, I discovered where the energy was coming from. A lunch-time concert of baroque music had just finished and it hadn't just charged up the church, it had given a boost to the energy of the whole area.

Back at the office, I found that a ley to the church (the NE-SW diagonal of the 8-point Earthstar) passed through the corner of the building and was positively vibrant with energy.

Colin Bloy often said that music had the power to re-build the ley network of the country. He told the tale of an experiment he had conducted in a Sussex field, using a tape (this was before CD's, i-pods and mp3 players) of Benedictine chants.

Within half an hour of playing the music, the energy pattern of the cathedral where it was recorded, had implanted itself on the field and could be dowsed quite clearly, having connected itself into the local energy centres. It took over a week to fade away.

The ringing of church bells has a similar effect, I am told. They can cleanse and sanctify the energies of a landscape.

So if you find a place that makes you want to sing, don't hold back, you may be re-energising the leys for miles around.

Tai Chi and Chi Gung

Performing Tai Chi or Chi Gung at sacred sites also boosts its energies, not to mention your own.

It plugs you into the energy of the place, the life-force of the land, and you become your own power-point. Try it. It is a great way to consciously heal the Earth whilst doing yourself a bit of good.

The return of the Grail Maidens

Traditionally, the Grail Maidens were the guardians of the sacred waters of life and the voices of the oracles of Britain.

They were essentially spirits of place at springs, wells, streams, lakes, ponds and rivers, but they may have had human counterparts who acted as guardians and oracles for them. Their story is told in The Elucidation, a foreword to Chretien de Troyes Grail Romance, Perceval.

The tale makes it very clear that the Grail Maidens were, and still are, the guardians of the grail and keepers of the "waters of life" a term which encompasses the esoteric life force, not just the physical waters.

The wasteland of the grail legends was created when the Grail Maidens withdrew from the world and were seen no more.

The abundance of nature diminished and the voices of the oracles of the shrines were heard no more.

Based on my own experiences with the Grail Maidens, or spirits of place at our Holy Wells, it is my belief they are returning and being seen again at their springs, wells, ponds, streams and lakes.

So whenever you are visiting such places, offer a blessing to the Grail Maidens and welcome their return. It marks the beginning of the healing of the wasteland.

What not to do

There is a saying:

"Leave nothing but footsteps.

Take nothing but photographs or memories."

It says it all.

Please don't leave candle wax, crystals, or any other bits and pieces.

If the site is a truly magical spot, let it remain unspoilt for others to enjoy.

Chapter Twenty Three

The Way of the Ley - Geosophy

The process you are opening yourself to on your pilgrimages along the leys, is called Geosophy, a word that derives from the Greek and simply means the wisdom of the Earth. Geo means Earth and Sophia is the Greek Goddess of Wisdom, who in many ways is synonymous with the Holy Spirit and The Earth Spirit.

The wisdom of the Earth is encoded in our sacred sites and is accessible to all who seek it with the right intent.

The Way of the Ley is the way of the mystic and the Gnostic.

It may even be the most ancient form of gnosis.

As the veteran ley expert Jimmy Goddard has stated, the lost science underlying the ley system is evidence of the Hidden Unity that links all life on Earth, to its source.

Follow the spiritual paths of our sacred landscape, walking in the old pathways and visiting places of knowledge and power are the first steps in understanding Geosophy, the wisdom of the Earth and our place on it.

Treat this as an act of pilgrimage, rather than just a jolly jaunt. Tread the old ways with an open heart and open mind.

Since we are part of the Earth Spirit and live within in it, the collective consciousness is out there in the landscape, all around us, not just within us.

It's a visionary and mythic landscape.

I can't guarantee you'll glimpse it in your travels. That depends on you. But knowingly or otherwise, you'll be travelling through it on a kind of urban vision quest.

You'll be a traveller in the vast mystery of the divine, the sacred landscape, the hidden unity where Heaven meets Earth.

If the forces of creation and life force of the planet actually do flow through these channels, sooner or later, you will feel it.

Go with the flow.

Plug yourself into the cosmic mains.

Become conscious of your light body.

Tread the paths of Earth Light and Star Light.

You walk the Earth, but you are a child of the stars.

The Great Mystery

I am the divinity within all things,
I am here within you
And within your family
And within your neighbours
And within your friends and enemies
Within your domestic animals
And within all the wild beasts of the Earth
Within your rivers and seas
Within your land, your plants, your trees
Within the air that you breathe and the food that you eat
I have always been here
But some do not see me
Look for me and I will open your eyes to a new world
Open your hearts to me in all you see around you
And I will open the gates of heaven on Earth to you
You enter it not in the flesh
But in the spirit
And the spirit you enter it in is mine
The Holy Spirit
The Spirit of Love
The Spirit of Wisdom

Adapted from Earthstars 1990

Blessings

For those inclined to bless places they visit,
here are some simple suggestions.

On arrival
Spirits of this sacred place
We bless and honour you
We come in the spirit of peace
And love
Give us protection, inspiration
Or healing
Each to our needs

On leaving
Spirits of this sacred place
We go now in peace
As in peace we came
We thank you for the experiences
We have enjoyed here
Until we meet again
May you be blessed by the Sun Moon and stars above
The Earth below
And by the turning wheels of the seasons throughout the years

A blessing for healng the Earth
We bless the guardians, gods, goddesses
and spirits of this sacred place
May healing be done here in accordance with divine will
May the power flow from this place
to connect with other sacred sites
And to spread a network of light, life, love, joy and healing
across our city, our country, our planet
May this power of peace and love be felt in the hearts
minds and souls of all people

Blessing for wells, springs, streams, ponds, lakes, rivers and fountains

We bless and honour the Grail Maiden of this well
(or spring, or whatever)
And invite her to return as guardian
of the sacred waters
May the waters of life and inspiration flow freely here
May the voice of the oracle be once again heard here
And may the Grail Maidens be seen here
May the wasteland be healed and restored
So we may live in harmony
with the abundance of nature's gifts

Blessing for world healing
Bless this centre of divine power
May its energies be restored to their full power and glory
Balanced in perfect harmony with divine will
May they flow forth from here
Carrying the power of light, life, peace, love and joy
To the hearts minds and souls of all mankind
May they heal humanity
May they heal the Earth
May the divisions between the worlds of man
nature spirit and divinity be healed
So that all the life forms that share this wonderful planet
may live in harmony

Shorter version
May the division between the worlds of humanity
nature and spirit be healed
So that all the life forms that share this wonderful planet
may live in harmony

Light Body meditation

Visualise yourself standing in a column of light
that shines vertically down on you.
Be aware that its point of origin is the heart of the universe.
Let the light shine into you as well as on you.
As you breathe in, draw the light into every cell of your being.
Start at your head and breathe the light into every cell of your brain.
Breathe it down into your lungs and heart.
Breathe it down into your fingertips
So that it shines out of your hands like healing rays.
Breathe it down into the tips of your toes.
Let it heal you.
Let it energise you.
Let it nourish you.
Until you are fully aware that your true essence
is as a being of light.
Not simply a physical being.
Then visualize the column of light shining down
through you into the centre of the Earth,
Where the molten white-hot core of our planet
burns like an inner sun.
Be aware that you stand between the heart of the Earth
and the heart of the Universe.
That you connect the two through your heart.
Radiate their healing light and power out from your heart
to connect all things, all people, in unity, light and love.
Hold that moment for as long as you like.
Then slowly reverse the visualisation to end.

Be aware that you carry these connections within you,
at all times, even in daily life.

**"From the stars we came.
To the stars we will return."**

210

**Further copies of this book are available on line
as a downloadable e book or paperback**

**Search the title or the author
on www.lulu.com**

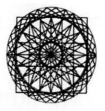

EARTHSTARS PUBLISHING
London N14 6LP

www.earthstars.co.uk

Index

214

Lightning Source UK Ltd.
Milton Keynes UK
UKOW05f0142161113

221198UK00003B/181/P